Successful Irish Businesswomen

Maxine Jones

THE MERCIER PRESS

The Mercier Press Limited
P.O. Box 5, 5 French Church Street, Cork *and*
24 Lower Abbey Street, Dublin 1

© Maxine Jones, 1992

ISBN 1-85635-030-4

A CIP catalogue record for this book
is available from the British Library

To Anna

Printed in Ireland by Colour Books Ltd.

Contents

Introduction

Only in the past twenty years have women in Ireland, and indeed elsewhere in Europe, begun to make any impact on the business world, despite the management skills they have shown for generations in running homes and looking after families.

Although various organisations have heightened awareness of the problem, women and their work, both in and out of the home, tend to be trivialised. Photographs of women are conspicuously absent on the business pages of newspapers, for example, yet are used in abundance elsewhere, often merely to brighten up the page.

Issues which are of particular interest to women are seen as marginal. Newspapers may offer a women's page, but there is the implication that the rest of the newspaper is for men. The bland and obvious assertion that women make up half the population is heard again and again, as if people still need reminding of the fact.

One anomaly which still exists in Ireland crops up at the registration of a birth. Only the father's occupation is requested. No space is allocated on the form for that of the mother. Future historians will find no record here of the Irish businesswoman.

Many of the women in this book are weary of going over the same battlegrounds. They are in fact too busy with their own enterprises. Yet their reason for participating was often that they felt they should stand up and be counted, for the sake of other women.

Part of a tiny minority, the Irish businesswoman is gradually finding a voice which is being picked up in government. Incidents of blatant discrimination in Irish law are being addressed, at least on the employment front. On the social and religious fronts, deeply seated prejudices, such as the ban on women priests, are only beginning to be discussed. The heated arguments which well up indicate that the battle will be long and fraught.

1992 saw the concerns of Irish women projected on to the world screen with widespread interest in the injunction preventing a fourteen-year-old rape victim from obtaining an abortion in England, and in the case of Bishop Eamonn Casey, who was revealed to have a child from an affair with an American woman. The hypocrisy inherent in Ireland's social structure with regard to women was made apparent to all.

On the other hand, there is a strong feeling of optimism among many women and men in Ireland, a sense that a more egalitarian society is on the way, where both sexes can fulfil their potential according to their individual inclinations rather than through conforming to male or female stereotypes.

The symbol of this optimism comes in the person of Ireland's first female president, Mary Robinson. She is carrying out her role so well that a veil has been drawn over the large part that chance played in her election. The principal contender, Brian Lenihan, a Fianna Fáil politician of the old guard, lost the faith of the electorate when he was accused of unethical tactics in trying to establish his party in government several years before. The third contender, Austin Currie, was from the north of Ireland, and thus the victim of another set of prejudices. Although Mary Robinson had strong support amongst many throughout her whole campaign, it is probably fair to say that most of the electorate got better than it deserved.

The picture in Ireland today is much less bleak than it was. Up until 1975, it was illegal for young women to be apprenticed. Up until 1973, women were sacked from public service when they married.

Legislative change has come about through the Commission on the Status of Women, set up in March 1970. The resulting Beere Report set out 68 recommendations for improving the lot of women in key areas, including the business world. The Council for the Status of Women, which now comprises over 80 women's organisations, was set up to ensure that those recommendations were implemented.

Though a step in the right direction, the recommendations did not go far enough to meet the needs of working women today. More than 600 submissions have been made to the Second Commission on the Status of Women, which is to publish its full report at the end of 1992.

Business opportunities and earning potential for women still lag behind those of men, despite laws passed in the 1970s to boost women's work prospects – the 1974 Anti-Discrimination Pay Act and the 1977 Employment Equality Act, which set up the Employment Equality Agency.

Equal pay has not yet been achieved. In June 1991, women's average earnings in Irish industry amounted to only 61% of men's average industrial earnings. Equality of opportunity is also a long way off.

Bernadette Forde of the Employment Equality Agency feels that, fifteen years after the first equality legislation, things have not moved far enough. She cites the electronics industry as an example of 'a new, clean industry where the old norms are perpetuating themselves. Only 3% of managerial positions in this area are filled by women, whereas 70% of operatives are women. Things may change but in ten years, not in two. On entering the open market in 1992, Ireland was still following the old pattern.'

The pattern is that women still fill only 10% of all management positions, but 73% of clerical positions. In local authorities, 99% of all junior grades are held by women, less than 7% of middle to senior management posts and no top level posts at all.

'Progress is slow, but as women stay longer in the workforce it is hoped they will gradually rise to the more senior posts,' says Bernadette Forde.

Stereotypes about work suitable for men and women are also being perpetuated. In the new commercial broadcasting sector, for example, 93% of technical jobs are held by men.

In 1990, Ireland's training and employment authority, FÁS, initiated a Positive Action Programme for Women, aimed at encouraging participation in male-dominated areas. FÁS, however, is no exception to the rule that women barely feature on the boards of state-sponsored bodies. Of its 18 board members, only one is a woman.

'The difficulty in enforcing equality legislation is reflected in the take-up of subjects at secondary level,' argues Bernadette Forde. 'According to a Department of Education report, in 1988, 90% of applied maths exam candidates were boys, as were 91% of engineering and 97% of technical drawing candidates. At the same time, 91% of home economics entrants were female. At third level, the picture is similar: 85% of engineering entrants are male, while 86% of social science entrants are female. Young people coming on stream into employment today are still likely to take up traditionally male or female jobs.'

Patrick Nolan of the Department of the Taoiseach admits that the pattern of female employment needs to be altered: 'This is one of the issues the Second Commission on the Status of Women will be looking at. We have been impressed by the number of submissions by members of the public and will be taking them into account in our recommendations. We will be addressing the problem of getting women into decision-making posts generally and giving them access to more business posts. It is encouraging that the number of young women on business studies courses is now on a par with boys.

'In 1972, when the First Commission reported, there was no enterprise culture,' he continued. 'There was no emphasis on women starting their own business or taking leading positions in business houses. The difficulty women have in reaching the top jobs is indicative of the problems they face in a lot of other areas.

'In the public sector where there are clear promotions paths it is hard enough, but in the private sector it is probably harder. Here, personal contacts are vital and women are denied a lot of these through the lack of old school or golf club connections, for example. One of the recommendations the Commission has already made in its first statement is that no lottery funding should go to clubs that discriminate against women.'

Network is an organisation for women in business, specifically aimed at providing the equivalent of 'old school connections'. 'We provide a grapevine which women can tap into and share their experience and expertise,' says Network Chairwoman Marion Creeley.

'Women come up against a corporate "glass ceiling". They get so far but no further, as if there were some invisible barrier. Network helps counteract the bias against women in the hierarchical structure of big business.

'Network has more than 400 members nationwide in manufacturing, retail, finance, communications and the media. Half run their own businesses, accounting for a total turnover of £30 million a year and employing over 2,000 workers. On the banking and managerial side, Network members account for budgets of around £100 million and employ approximately 9,000 people.

'Network is building up a more public profile and offering guidelines to the Government. We have produced a study on the attributes of board members. We have also prepared a comparative report on the effects of positive action programmes abroad to see what measures might be of benefit to this country.

'Most of all, we hope to inspire others, especially young people. Women have made substantial gains in business and there is a lot to be built upon. It is a positive stage to be at,' Marion Creeley concluded.

One of the barriers to women setting up their own businesses has been the reluctance of banks to lend them money. As women climb the ladder within banking organisations, this is changing. Another force for change is Women's World Banking, which is currently working to establish itself in Ireland. Founded in 1979, WWB lends money to prospective businesswomen with no collateral.

'In the past ten years, WWB has focused on access to credit,' says New York chairwoman, Nancy Barry. 'In the next ten, we will be helping women find investors for their businesses, helping them to get more training and develop larger markets and better communication networks.'

Most of the women featured in this book have set up their own businesses. Discouraged by the general attitudes of employers, they preferred to work for themselves. Some, victims of the marriage bar, had no choice. Others considered it the only way to accommodate work and family.

While being a working father is not seen as a handicap, a working mother sets off alarm signals for many employers. Women supply the domestic back-up for the majority of men at work, yet there is a gaping hole when it comes to support systems for women at work.

The first priority for most working mothers is to employ a child minder. Yet the Government does not consider this a tax-deductible expense. Few companies have followed the lead of Aer Rianta, Radio Telefís Éireann, Bord Telecom, and the Bank of Ireland in setting up workplace crèches.

In 1990, a seminar on childcare provision, organised jointly by the Employment Equality Agency and the EC Network on Childcare, concluded: 'The provision of childcare facilities to working parents is becoming a key issue for the labour market of the 1990s. If the Irish economy is to keep pace with that of the post-1992 European Community, its childcare provision will have to be radically improved.'

The urgency has arisen, not because in all fairness women should have the chance to work if they choose, but because they are going to be needed to fill a shortfall in the workforce. By the year 2025 it is expected that the population of Europe will have fallen by 2% and the proportion of those aged over sixty-five will have risen to more than 20%. Employers will be looking for new sources of labour.

While it is difficult to imagine a labour shortage in Ireland, European trends will be reflected as workers are attracted out of the country under the new conditions of free mobility of labour. It is only a matter of time before the patterns already emerging in Europe and the United States appear in Ireland. Ireland has the advantage of being able to follow the examples set in other countries when it comes to increasing childcare provision.

Already 23.6% of married women participate in the labour force, compared with 5.42% in 1961. Even in the year 1987–8, when the participation rate for both men and women in general declined, the number of married women in the workforce continued to increase. In 1990, 23% of mothers with children under nine were working and the greater proportion of these had children under four years of age.

The women interviewed in this book have little in common except that they belong to the minority of women who have made it in business. Yet certain traits emerge. Those who are mothers feel that having children has a positive overall effect on their work. Not only does the need to provide for them help concentrate their efforts, but time spent with the children enables them to switch off totally from work and retain a healthy perspective.

The consensus is that their children's lives are also enriched by the insight they gain into business through their mother's activities. They are also spared the influence of the sexual stereotyping of earlier generations.

The women interviewed share a sense of humour and a lack of pomposity. They are all energetic, enthusiastic, and engaging. They have recognised their strengths and are enjoying putting them to work for themselves. Several made the point that the resources women have shown over the years in the domestic sphere – tenacity, scrupulousness, the ability to concentrate on several things at once, ease in communicating, and a talent for lateral thinking – are exactly the skills needed to be successful in business. Recognising the underdeveloped talents of many women, they show a keenness to promote them within their own organisations.

Enjoyment is paramount for them. They see their work as fun rather than a chore. Though working long hours, they all place value on activities outside work and on making time for family and friends. They seem to epitomise the maxim, 'The more you do, the more you can do'.

These women have worked out their own values along the way. They see success not purely in material terms, but in terms of self-fulfilment and the satisfaction that comes from proving they can achieve their aims. They have put a new meaning on the term 'business success'.

All the women interviewed responded with grace and honesty. Two more, Gillian Bowler and Carol Moffett, agreed to be interviewed but their schedules did not fit in with the deadline for delivery of the book. Gillian Bowler started Budget Travel from a one-room basement in Baggot Street, Dublin, when she was twenty-one years old. Her achievements have received much media attention. Budget Travel is now the largest travel agency in the country with a turnover of around £20 million, and 60 employees.

Gillian is convinced anything is possible if you have the will to attain it. 'The vague urge to work for yourself and make lots of money, is a recipe for disaster. But if you have determination and see a clear path ahead, then you can find solutions to practically anything,' she said.

She believes that women are well able to overcome any prejudices which may still exist against them: 'In the sense that I believe women should extend and fulfil themselves, I am a feminist,' she said. 'But while I agree that in some areas it is harder for a woman to succeed than in others, I believe that if a woman is determined, then her sex isn't and shouldn't be a stumbling block.'

Carol Moffett is Managing Director of Moffett Engineering in Clontibret, Co. Monaghan. Engineering is an area in which women are only just beginning to make inroads. Carol would have been a rarity when, in 1972, at the age of nineteen, she took over her father's small engineering firm. She has since built the firm up into one of the most innovative engineering manufacturers in Ireland, exporting machinery of its own design all over the world.

This book highlights the achievements of certain women in certain areas. The purpose is not to labour any particular point nor to substantiate any particular theory about women in business, it is just to let a few of them tell their own stories and give them the chance to stand up and be counted.

~ *One* ~

Freda Hayes

Chief Executive, Blarney Woollen Mills

BLARNEY Woollen Mills started from small beginnings – a thatched cottage on wheels selling souvenirs to tourists. The enterprise is now virtually an empire, embracing knitwear manufacturing, retailing and tourism. It is still based in Blarney, now housed in a massive old mill, and has three shops in Dublin, two in Killarney and two in the UK. It also supplies wholesale in Ireland and eight other countries.

The fourteen-year-old girl who helped out her father in the thatched cottage is now chief executive of the company. Freda Hayes summarises a growth process which has spanned twenty-five years.

'You start off in one business and it branches out. We started in a small retailing business which was seasonal because it was tourist-only related. That necessitated keeping ourselves busy in the winter so we developed a hand-knitting company. We had hand-knitters from one end of Ireland to the other, four or five hundred of them. Eventually we developed from hand-knitting into automated machinery and then into the knitwear business proper. We went on to develop the retail side and bought the Martin Manning woollen mills in Blarney, which had gone into receivership.'

The thatched cottage is now a museum piece in the main mill complex. 'It was a tiny cottage on wheels. We didn't have money to buy property or anything like that. We started from nothing at all. It was my father's vision. He saw an opportunity in the number of tourists who came to Blarney. He was always into something or other and this was just another one of the things he was going to try.'

Freda's father, Christy Kelleher, had worked in the old mill until 1951. He then took a job in insurance and ran the shop as a sideline 'because there were many more mouths to feed at home'. Freda comes in the middle of seven children. She has three older brothers and two sisters and a brother who are younger. All are now involved in the company.

'I left school to work in the shop. If there were six or

seven in the shop, we had a crowd. I did everything from the buying to the merchandising to the selling.' The turnover was tiny, but the business was successful.

Freda was always the boss. 'That's the way it fell. The three older boys were already working and I was next down the line. It wasn't that I showed any great prowess as a budding entrepreneur at the age of sixteen.'

Freda does not regret that her schooling was cut short. 'At the end of the day I've learnt an awful lot from the school of life. At forty years of age now, I've had the bones of twenty-five years in business. I've made all the mistakes and thankfully come out the other side.'

The Martin Manning mill in Blarney went into receivership in 1975. 'It was around the time of Ireland's entry into the EEC and the traditional textile industry just couldn't compete with imports,' Freda explained. 'It was a really big old mill and nobody wanted it. At one stage it had employed about 1,000 people, but had been running down slowly. When it eventually closed, it was still employing 200 or 300. When I was going to school most people's fathers worked in the mill. Everybody in the area had a connection with it.'

The idea that Freda's family should buy the mill was greeted with horror by their bankers and professional advisers. 'They all thought we were mad.'

She is still trying to come to terms with her father's death in 1991. 'He enjoyed every minute of the company. He had a way with people, he knew everyone. He didn't get involved in the nitty gritty running of the company, he always left that to me, but he was a fantastic ambassador for Blarney.'

Freda's mother stayed at home. 'It was a traditional family. She would do the washing and cooking and try to make sure that, however the business was doing, we were all properly looked after.'

It was her mother's input that had got the business started in the first place. 'When my father was starting in business it was my mother's savings that got him going. They would have amounted to £200 and were used to build the original cottage. As was the tradition, all his wages went to his wife to rear the children. He had money for a newspaper or whatever. There's an old saying, "She'd mind mice at a crossroads", which fitted my mother. She was very careful about where to spend the money and on what. She would travel a long way to get a bargain.'

Buying the mill put the family into the major league. 'We had to find £70,000 to buy the mill and we couldn't get a loan at the time because nobody thought it was a good idea. There were seven of us in the family so we all took out loans of £10,000 each, some of us using our homes as guarantees.'

They did very little with the mill when they first got it. 'There we were with the mill but with no money to do anything with it. We opened just one side of a room in this huge monstrosity of a building. We bought black refuse sacking in a huge wide roll and simply dropped it as a partition.

'We had a knitwear factory up the road by this time but we didn't move that down for a good few years. We also had a second shop in the village. We went into a business we didn't really know much about. Sometimes I look back and think if we had been too knowledgeable at the beginning, we would never have done it.

'My father was a born optimist. He didn't really need much materially himself. He was quite prepared to take a risk. He didn't even question it. He enjoyed looking at the company working.'

Developing the mill took time. 'We had so much space. We opened a hotel in the mill. There are still floors in it we haven't developed. We had to wait to make money to reinvest. We didn't have capital. My father always hated too much borrowing. He was a visionary. The mill had captured his imagination. In times before, there'd been the workers' entrance and there'd been the main entrance, which was forbidden to people like us. The first thing he did was knock down the gates and open the whole thing up. He could envisage what we have today. He could see that in 1975.'

Freda sees the success of Blarney Woollen Mills as dependent on good team work. 'Every entrepreneur needs somebody to carry out their vision. None of us has every quality, the ability to have the vision, take the risks and be disciplined enough to carry it all through. You need other people around you in a business. I'd still be the major risk-taker in our family. I still like to move on and move on.

'Now it's easier. As we've grown as a company, we've built up a good team of people. Ours is a very female oriented company. We have to watch it that we don't go too female oriented and become sexist in the other direction.'

The company has 350 employees. 'It's taken us twenty-five years. Somebody said to me once, "It's easy for you, you're big." I said, "Well we didn't start big". If you go through the history of all the major companies, whether it's Smurfit or Waterford Glass or any of them, they all started the same way, maybe not in 1975, but in 1925. Every company starts with one person's idea.'

The family opened its first shop in Dublin in 1983. 'My father was very Blarney. He was born and raised there and was very cautious about moving to Dublin. I suppose it's an old Irish thing that he always wanted to own his own patch. Most high street properties in Dublin at that time were only available on leasehold.

'We went into a very small shop in Duke Street just to test it out. That was hard enough grafting. In hindsight now, maybe we'd have been better off in a different location. But it didn't lose us money and we learnt a lot from it. With that experience behind us, we moved on to Nassau Street about three or four years later.'

Freda's father had always encouraged her and pushed her forward, even as a small child. 'If politicians ever came to Blarney, he'd always say, "Get out and meet them".' Freda herself is interested in politics but would have no interest at all in public life.

'I'm a member of a political party and I take a keen interest in politics. I think that in a serious business, a large business where you're employing a lot of people, you have to take a broader view of what's happening in Ireland. I'm involved in all sorts of things. I'm in the Chamber of Commerce, on the national executive of the FIE (Federation of

Irish Employers), have various tourism involvements, and am on the board of Córas Tráchtála, our export board. They've all helped me to see the larger picture.

'They take time and involve a lot of hassle and sometimes I wish I was back doing a host of other things. But at the same time, from a family business point of view, it's essential that you do that, otherwise you'd get tunnel vision.'

Time is at a premium for Freda. 'As a woman trying to manage home and business, time is a very important commodity. My son, Ronan, is sixteen. There is a certain price to be paid. If you want to work, then you must put in the infrastructure at home. Ronan is my son from my first marriage, and being that involved in business can be very trying on a marriage. I'm not saying that business was the reason the marriage broke down, but business shapes your character to be very independent and that can make marriage more difficult.

'I was married first when I was twenty-two. He was a local boy. It just didn't work out. I got married again five years ago now. My husband works for Guinness Peat Aviation. He's very involved with GPA and travels all over the world. I say to people, it's a marriage made in heaven. He comes home at weekends and I have all the freedom to do my own thing. It's the kind of marriage that works for me. When you're running your own company there's no way you can be a nine to five person.'

THE BLARNEY success story was no clear run. In 1986 profits plummeted by 80%. 'It was the time of the Gaddafi crisis. We were dependent on American visitors. We were nearly wiped out in one year after all our years in the business. We had to start really developing a home market, which we've now done very successfully. That's why we expanded in Dublin. It means we now have a very balanced trade.

'Opportunities are always presenting themselves. I'm in favour of moving on. We just this week bought a second shop in Killarney. We're expanding our knitwear retailing side, so I can see us doing a number of things throughout

Ireland. On the hotel side, we've learnt a lot in the last few years and if a good opportunity presented itself there, we might expand. You can't do everything. At the end of the day, the important thing is that we keep our eye on the ball and maintain what we have now in a cost-effective manner.'

What they have now, as well as the Killarney shops, are the Kilkenny and Blarney Woollen Shops in Nassau Street, Dublin, and Club Tricot in Grafton Street, Dublin. 'We specialise in quality Irish goods, which makes us different from the other stores. I would hope we'd never change from that.' They opened their shop in Windsor, England, five years ago and one in Cambridge two years ago. 'The economy in England isn't exactly thriving, but we're hanging in there.'

Russia may be the next move. 'I'm just back from three days in Moscow to see what opportunities are there for our knitwear products. I suppose what happens when you get to a certain size is that opportunities present themselves a lot quicker. People come all the time saying, have a look at this. You haven't time to look at everything and you must be careful not to jump in too quickly.

'In the last four or five years we've been well established in Irish retailing terms as one of the major players. You have to watch as well that you don't overstretch yourself. I'm still careful about our borrowings and things like that. There's only a certain amount you can do then unless you take in equity and I don't have any plans for that at the moment.

'Last year was a tough year. In any business you have to be successful enough to ride out the bad years. Inevitably they come every few years and if you're in any way financially unstable, a bad year will kill you.'

FREDA FINDS working as a family has more advantages than drawbacks. Her two sisters, a sister-in-law, her brothers and a brother-in-law are all closely involved in the business. 'It's very diverse so everyone has their own different sphere. The main advantages are commitment, loyalty, and common work ethics. In general it works very well. I think a lot of problems with family business happen with the next generation, who are not so closely related – when you're getting into cousins. The history of other family businesses can tell you a lot. We try and encourage all our offspring, of which there are now twenty-four, to look elsewhere. It would be very difficult with such a large family to let them all in. If you allowed one in, you'd have to allow them all.'

As the principal players are still so young, there is no urgency to look for successors. Freda could only envisage the children entering the company if they had already gone their own ways and gained experience in an area relevant to the workings of the company. 'If their field is in the hotel industry, we could be dying to get our hands on them, once they've proved themselves outside the company. It would be no good for them to offer them the easy way out. They would have terrible lives. So we tell them!'

FREDA'S OVERALL philosophy as far as work is concerned is 'You have to have fun. You have to put things in place and make sure you have time for your company, for your family, for yourself.'

For eight years after her first marriage broke up, Freda and her son were on their own. 'It meant starting all over again for me. Being a separated woman in Ireland and rearing a son isn't always easy. But of course being financially independent I was luckier than most women. I could start again and go out and buy myself a three-bedroomed semi-detached house and get a mortgage.'

Even then it wasn't so easy. 'The building society turned me down first time unless my husband would sign. I said, "I'm separated. I don't have a relationship with my husband. I cannot get in touch with him". We nearly came to blows.' This was twelve years ago. Freda had been running her own business for thirteen years.

'I never realised I'd have that problem, but I eventually got my mortgage and off I went. Very few women would be as lucky. Maybe lucky is the word. I know how difficult it would be for a woman with two or three children to walk away and not have a job. It would be impossible.'

Working for herself has allowed for flexibility as well as financial independence. 'When you work for yourself, you have long hours, but you also have freedom. If your child is sick in the morning you can go in later. A woman who wants to succeed in a multinational organisation hasn't the freedom to say she can't come in if she has problems. It may affect her career.'

FREDA UNWINDS by doing 'the odd bit of aerobics. The difficult thing is to get into a pattern because I'm away so much. My husband sails, so at weekends in the summertime we go out on to the sea. I like to read my newspapers, and to sip a beer or a glass of wine. I find it easy to switch off. I can work in the office until midnight some nights but the minute I go home I forget about it. You go in, you start dinner and make time for your child.

'Women are good at taking pressure. We are not so worried about our public persona, which takes a bit of pressure off us. We're inclined to be more sensitive. We feel problems approaching and take action before they reach a point where they could cause real trouble. I also think we can get closer to people, so we get feedback in a more natural way.

'My mind is always in ten different places at once. I have to keep a handle on all different aspects of the business. I could be sitting in a hotel management meeting on menus and wine one minute and have to go up to the knitwear factory the next. But I don't have any problem with that. I've worked in all areas of the company as it has developed.

'I'd hate to be totally wound down. I'd certainly like to be able to travel more and take more time off. But at the same time, I hate being away more than a week at any one time.

'As the company gets bigger I have less time. But I have very good people. The important thing is to have good communications. Whether it's bad or good I want to be sure they're not just telling me what they think I want to hear. It's important to me to have a relationship with them where they can be honest and tell me if I've made a mistake or if they've made one. I can cope with anything once I know.'

~ *Two* ~

Rhona Teehan

**Owner of Suesey Street night club,
The Trocadero restaurant
and Café Caruso, Dublin**

'I'M A GENIUS,' says Rhona Teehan typing the last word of a letter disputing the high cost of music royalties paid by nightclubs. 'I haven't typed for twenty years.'

Her glee is infectious and it soon becomes clear that Rhona Teehan's unaffected manner and sense of fun have been instrumental in 'getting people through the door' and establishing her nightclub and restaurants as among the most popular in Dublin.

She is very much at the centre of things. It is her personality which helps draw people back, and which was responsible for getting the venues established in the first place. In setting up Suesey Street, she would literally go around the pubs in Dublin and gather the crowds, leading them, pied piper-like, back to her club.

'My first image is probably as a Leeson Street club owner,' she says. 'It's an image I could do without, mostly because the image of Leeson Street has changed. The people going there are younger and I'm getting more mature. A lot of people would associate me with the Trocadero now. In fact, the younger population think that it's always been mine. Only the older people realise it's been there for thirty-five years.'

At forty-two, Rhona's fresh complexion and bright eyes seem to belie the fact that she spends most nights in clubs and restaurants, often stays up until three or four in the morning and smokes and drinks as much as she pleases.

She puts this down to her general attitude to life. 'I've no worries, really. Or I just don't have the personality to accommodate worry. I don't worry. I have a good life and I enjoy my life. I appreciate it.'

However, the nightclub image is beginning to pall. 'I'm very tired with Leeson Street now. I find myself going in and looking at my watch every fifteen minutes wondering when I'll be of no value and I can go home.' The answer to what she does there is brief: 'I drink champagne.' She knows most of the customers and will chat to them. 'In fact, if I dropped out I'd probably miss it badly.

'It's good that I go in, not just for the customers but also for the staff. I have a manageress. If I backed out, I'd lose touch with her.'

Her relationship with her staff is a good one, and has been an important element in the success of her ventures. 'I've never had big lucky touches in business, but I've had enormous good fortune with the people who work for me. I don't do much work, but I stay real close.

'It's very hard to think of my business as being real business. I can't imagine that a man would have adopted my style. And it wouldn't work for him either. I'm like a clan head and the people who work for me for any length of time are part of that clan. I would think that the principal people who work for me see themselves with me for ever. If there was going to be a break away or if anything happened to me they would inherit some of my business. I see them in the same context as family.'

RHONA LEFT DUBLIN at eighteen to go to America, where she attended junior college and worked in a factory at night. She returned to Dublin and left again at twenty-one, this time for London.

'I got a job in the Playboy Club and I worked as a croupier in other places as well. I made piles of money – and spent it all. I bought a house with a boyfriend over there. It was a beautiful house on ten acres in Kent, built in 1484. I had a wonderful six years – the last three in particular. We were very rich, but we spent huge amounts of money and the whole lot went. We ended up split up and I was back in Dublin with nothing at all.'

Rhona got a job in the office of a building and plumbing suppliers, earning £28 a week. 'I'll never forget standing at a bus-stop in Terenure. It was November, cold, raining, quarter past eight in the morning. I just started whingeing. I stood there and bawled my eyes out.

'I had no money and I was back home. Most of my friends were married and getting on with their lives and I felt I had nothing. I was like Cinderella. I couldn't live on the money I was earning. I was giving £10 to my mother, £10 for fares and had just £8 left.'

The turning-point came after she had been home about three weeks. 'I went down Leeson Street with my sister. As soon as I walked in I thought, "This is the life, this is more like what I'm used to". So I got a job working in Bojangles for £5 a night. And that was the start of me.'

RHONA TEEHAN GREW UP in Terenure. Her father died when she was eleven and her mother took in lodgers. She is the youngest of five and has three brothers and a sister.

'My mother was very demanding and very appreciative. Money was tight and we had to contribute to the upkeep of the house. My father had been a civil servant and we lived in a nice area. My mother was ambitious. We could have owned a house in somewhere like Crumlin, but my mother wouldn't have us live in Crumlin, so we rented a house in Terenure. When my father died she got £1,000, a year's salary, and that was it.

'I missed him dreadfully at the time. He was very warm and good-humoured. After his death, my mother came into her own. She would have loved to have gone out and earned a living, but she couldn't, she had five kids, and anyway she was intimidated by my father who reckoned he was better educated and brighter. She had just a basic education and was full of energy. When she took in lodgers, she found it very rewarding. She treated it like a business. When I first went into business she had lots of suggestions to make.

'I don't think I'd have been so single-minded about what I wanted if he had stayed alive. He would have wanted me to go to university and get a degree, and become a career woman, but probably not in this line.

'I have no regrets about not going to university. I can't understand people who do, and if they do they should go back. The idea that there might be a big gap because you didn't go to university is nonsense. There is nothing I particularly regret.'

Rhona is dismissive of the suggestion that her good looks might have guided her career path. 'I don't think my looks had any great influence on the road I took, certainly no more than anybody else. How you present yourself affects everybody's life. I was never stunning. I was always pleasant to look at. I never had the kind of face that a guy would be afraid to come over to or a girl would be jealous of. I was lucky. It was great. I had a friendly, pleasant, open face. But my looks wouldn't have dictated anything particular. There was no danger of being a Cindy Crawford or anything.'

ONCE SHE HAD TAKEN THE JOB in Bojangles, Rhona knew she was never going to work in an office again. 'It just wasn't going to work for me. I decided I was going to head into the restaurant business some way.

'I started going out with Pierre Doyle, who had opened a pool hall in St Stephen's Green. I asked him if I could open a coffee bar in the pool hall. That cost me £1,400. I'd eventually got £5,000 out of England when the house was sold, and I'd saved some.'

Rhona made the coffee bar a success by dint of hard work. 'I always liked working hard. I'd get up in the morning and go and buy the stuff for the sandwiches and work in the coffee bar all day. I made £100 a week there, which was a great jump from £28.'

Pierre Doyle then asked her to go and look at a nightclub with him. She went along and ended up buying 20% of it. 'That cost me £7,000. Then I was on my way. It had all happened within a year. I was now 28.'

Six months after opening the coffee bar, Rhona decided she was going to open a restaurant. She went to work in the kitchens of the prestigious Grey Door restaurant with the specific idea of learning the business. Then she set up Kilmartin's wine bar in Baggot Street with a friend, who still works with Rhona today. 'The partner I picked was wonderful. She educated me. She'd been a manageress at Murph's, a fashionable Dublin restaurant, since she was sixteen.'

Meanwhile, Pierre had decided to cut her out of the nightclub, just one of the 'ups and downs' of their eight-year relationship. 'What a schemer!' she says of him, but with good humour and admitting that they are still friends now.

Disappointed with what she saw as the paltry sum she got out of the nightclub, she was now sinking her energies into Kilmartin's. 'I had a real flair for the business. I love my own food. I'm not saying that my palette is terribly sophisticated or anything, but I just like food. I like eating. I tend to impose my own likes on the menus and on how things are cooked and it seems to suit a lot of people.

'I like cooking, but I don't do it any more, I haven't cooked for eight years. I eat in the restaurants every night. I'm not a weight gainer,' she says, spooning sugar freely into her coffee.

'When you have your own restaurant, you know your way round the menu. It's like eating at home. I had my dinner last night in the Trocadero with a couple of girlfriends. One of them had corned beef with cabbage and a huge big jug of parsley sauce and creamed potato. I had Irish stew and a big bowl of peas. I can go in there and eat the same sort of thing you'd eat at home. If I'm in the humour, I can eat something more sophisticated. I often find myself eating comfort food.'

RHONA COMES BACK TO THE POINT that she doesn't feel like a real businesswoman because what she does comes so naturally. 'Another thing that makes me feel I'm not a true businesswoman is that I can't bear to let go. I've only sold one business and that was Kilmartin's. I only sold that because it was too tiny to be viable when I went on to Leeson Street and then on to the Trocadero. My manageress was very anxious to buy it off me so I sold it to her.

'I bought Leeson Street and the Trocadero in the same year. I sold Kilmartin's. I never had a moment's doubt about any business. It never dawned on me that it wouldn't work. I think if you look at businesses that do fail, there's never a mystery. Things are up on the wall for anyone to see. I've never gone into a big gamble with anything I've opened. Anyone would have given it an 80% chance of success.'

The Leeson Street club was already up and running, under the name of Aphrodite's, when she bought it. 'I was still going out with Pierre at the time. He'd made an absolute fortune. He had subsequently bought Elizabeth's. I was working an eighteen-hour day at Kilmartin's. It was inhuman. I used to get up at half past five in the morning and start cooking. It was a little bistro. Then I'd go in and work it. We opened at 12.15 and last orders were at midnight. I'd come home at the end of the night and I'd say, "We had a great day today, we took £850". Pierre would say, "I didn't have such a great day, I only took two and a half grand".

'I got so jealous. I thought I've got to get back into this club business. I'd been trying to buy one club for a long time and every time we got close to the deal, the owner backed out and upped the price again. He had me driven crazy.

'Pierre met him in his nightclub one night and they started drinking and he told him, "You've no honour, you do a deal and then you back out". The guy turned round and said, "I do not. I will sell it". So Pierre said, "Put a price on it and don't be always changing your mind".' (In negotiating the sale of property, the selling price is never binding until a written agreement signed by both the vendor and purchaser specifying the price, property and parties, is drawn up.)

'Pierre phoned me up at four o'clock in the morning and said, "Do you still want this nightclub?" I said, "You know I do". And he said, "Well, it's £110,000". I said, "What?" I had started negotiating at £55,000. I asked for five minutes to think about it. I put the phone down and I rang him back about five minutes later and said, "I'll have it". I was already up mentally to £85,000 and if a Leeson Street venture is going to work, your £20,000 will be back in no time and if it's not going to work, it's not going to work at £85,000 or £110,000. It doesn't matter.'

Rhona then set about creating her clientèle. 'A huge amount of hard work went into establishing Suesey Street. I was in every pub every night, six nights a week, for a year and a half and I wasn't home before half-past five every morning. I'd go into Scruffy Murphy's pub and I'd walk up to people. I wouldn't remember their name but I'd have seen them somewhere, I'd been around town a long time. I'd say, "I haven't seen you in a while", and I'd buy them a drink. The guys did it, so I thought, "To hell with this, why can't I?"

'Then I got the most beautiful girl, I thought, in the whole country to work for me. She wouldn't have been the greatest worker in the world but she was exquisite. So I used to drag her into every pub in town with me. I'd do my walking round bit and end up talking to everyone in the bar and sure enough they came down.

'There was an advertising crowd and an RTE crowd. I was very friendly with Barry Devlin, Dermot Morgan, Pat Kenny, Shay Healy. They'd come in and Jean Foley, the manageress, really took care of them. She came on the scene about two years after I opened. They just made it their club and then I was away. I didn't have to do the grind any more.'

Rhona heard the Trocadero was available when a friend came up to her and asked her if she'd like it. 'I said I'd love it. I didn't ask if he meant to buy or rent it. I just wanted it, under any circumstances. I got it under a licence arrangement which is causing me great grief at the moment. I will resolve it but it's a big worry. If two people are going to court, one always loses.' Rhona was planning a High Court appeal against a judge's decision that she should move out of the premises. With twenty full-time staff at the Trocadero and having been there for seven years, she was going to fight her corner.

In her business dealings generally, Rhona says, she is not ruthless but she is certainly no soft touch. 'If I have someone working for me who's not fair, to the business, to me, to the others, I have no difficulty in the world in firing them. I'd tell them why. It would never be on a personal basis. I'd never take a notion against someone or a dislike of them and act on a thing like that, ever. If I have somebody working for me who I don't personally like very much, I will stay out of their way.'

Rhona is not in a managerial situation, neither does she interview staff. She has great faith in her managers, Robert Doggett and Jean Foley. 'Robert built up the Trocadero almost single-handedly. I'm very much just an owner, but I put in a tremendous amount of time keeping close to them. I would see myself as a support system for them.'

DESPITE SEVERAL LONG-TERM relationships, Rhona has never married. She says she has more energy and feels more inspired and productive when she is single than when she is going out with a man. At thirty-six, she discovered she was unable to have children. She would love to have had them and is hurt when people assume that she devalues motherhood and has put her career first.

'When I was living with the boyfriend in England, I really thought I was going to spend my life with him. We planned to have kids. I wanted to do everything. I wanted business and family. I wanted everything.

'Having said that, I've had a great life and I have a great life. It's very churlish of me to harp on about not having kids. I've had more than my share of luck in health and in other ways.'

Rhona knows a lot of women who have had children and brought them up on their own, often in adverse circumstances. She suspects some pregnancies were not as unplanned as the women claimed. 'People don't have accidents. Twentieth-century women who've been on the pill, who have a life style set up, they don't have accidents. They actually collude with the biological urge.'

Rhona no longer worries about not having children. 'The day I was forty, it was like that part of my life was over. It was as if someone had taken a weight off me and I was never to worry about it again. All I had to do was enjoy my life, take what I'd been given and make the best of it.'

Neither does she worry about not being married. 'All the rubbish you go through as a single woman – people say to you, "It's all right being single now but what about when you're forty?" Well here I am at forty-two and I couldn't give a monkey's about being on my own. Being married is no insurance policy. Health is worth anything.'

Rhona has a horror of people who take exercise too seriously, but keeps healthy herself through sports she enjoys. She hunts in the winter and has her own horse which she keeps in Kildare. She also plays a lot of golf in the summer. She lives in a 'huge big house' in Rathmines with a cat 'that came in off the street and adopted me'.

RHONA OPENED CAFÉ CARUSO in March 1991. 'I had a vision of it and it was great fun putting it together. I had a complete mental picture.'

The future offers several possibilities. 'I see myself either opening a unit this size every three years or going into the hotel business. I haven't quite made up my mind and I'll let it lead me along to some extent.

'I can feel a burst of energy on the way,' says Rhona. 'I split up with someone just last week, and I've got the urge to go again. It took me three years to find this place. I'd prefer to stay in Dublin. The other thing I'm very interested in is fast food franchise. There's great growth potential there. I'm a bit stretched owning three places that are all built around the personal touch.

'The criteria for a place that suits me are quite rigid. It has to be at a certain rent level. I've never stretched myself for money. I don't take financial risks any more. In the beginning I had to. The first year in Suesey Street, I lived on credit with suppliers and they were really good to me. I'd say to them "Your name's in the hat this week, you might get paid".'

Prices in her two restaurants are in the middle bracket. 'I have no aspirations to have an expensive restaurant. I get great reward value from coming into Café Caruso and seeing it full and everyone enjoying themselves. Or going into the Trocadero and seeing the great cross-section of customers. I have newspaper sellers who have been going in there for fifteen years and they eat the biggest meals I have ever seen.

'When I open, I totally forget about making a profit. My first thing is get people in the door. I don't overspend. A restaurant in your wildest dreams couldn't repay £1 million, for example.

'I'm always thinking of things to add without increasing price. I'm going to do everything I can for £25 to try and be as good as a £50 a head restaurant. Sometimes I can't do it. It has to be paper tablecloths, for example. But there are other things I can do. I can be welcoming, I can see that the staff are professional and know their job and I can give everyone in the house a drink on the house. That's not outside the budget.'

'I'D LOVE TO SEE every woman in the country go into business,' says Rhona with gusto. 'I think they're super at it. The big thing they lack is confidence. The things that men have been praised for as regards success, like being single-minded and concentrating on the success of the business, they're not always positive traits. Certainly in my business a man who came in every day intent on climbing the career ladder wouldn't be much use. He wouldn't think laterally enough, or be approachable enough and he wouldn't be sensitive to people. You've nothing if you don't have a customer. Women are great at all these things.'

Politics holds an attraction for Rhona, but she has as yet only flirted with the idea. 'Politics is a notion. For fun. What do you do when you're forty-five? But the reality of it would probably be a drag. And the lack of independence. And the frustration of trying to move things and nothing moves. That's the most fantastic part of being on my own and being relatively small. I make a decision and it's in effect within seven days.'

Most decisions are made in consultation with her managers Robert and Jean and her sister, Lynn, who is the paymaster. Rhona is happy to let her sister run the money side. 'Money bores me silly. I wouldn't count up the take, ever.'

She sometimes feels under pressure to apologise for being successful, especially when relating to men. 'People assume if you're successful you're going to be hard. I'm not desperately interested in money. I don't get along with big businessmen whose lives revolve round making money. I've no interest in them. They bore me. Business, in inverted commas, bores me.

'I want to go out with people I like gossiping with, playing golf with and getting drunk with, people who are like myself. But generally they don't have as much money as I have. You're walking on eggshells, without a doubt.' She regrets not being able to buy a man an expensive present, for example, for fear of bruising his ego.

'Women spend a lot of time and energy minding men's egos,' muses Rhona, 'especially their man. It's a shame. It's like living with a corn on your foot all your life.'

~ *Three* ~

Rose Wright

Director,
Leo Wright Group

AFTER A QUIET DRIVE through the village of Milltown-pass in Co. Westmeath, it is something of a shock to stumble upon a large car park in front of a vast factory which is literally buzzing and whirring with activity.

The spirit behind this enterprise is Rose Wright, who has been instrumental in turning her husband's small joinery business into one of the biggest in the county, with a work-force of more than one hundred. The company manufactures and installs timber and uPVC windows, doors, conservatories and stairs throughout Ireland, including the competitive Dublin market.

Rose is keen to stress that the success of the business is due to the hard work of both herself and her husband, though the vision and faith which propelled them on when things were tough seems to have come mainly from Rose.

ROSE IS ONE OF twelve children, six boys and six girls. Being among the older ones, she had early experience in organising and planning. She spent some of her early years in a convent where she developed a spiritual perspective which enables her to take a wider view of things. Inspirational mottos line her office wall. 'I look out and up, never down,' she maintains.

'I was in a Mercy convent. I learnt a lot. It did a lot for me, in my views of life and so on. I never regretted it. I only started to live when I left, but the build-up and the character forming happened while I was there. I left because it was very enclosed. I felt that I had a lot to give and didn't have the outlets.

'My mother was invalided with multiple sclerosis after my father's death in 1968 and there were young members of the family who needed care. I decided there was more to do out there.'

Rose began her working life as a national school teacher. She left the convent in June 1969 and started teaching in her local school. Her organisational ability soon had her running organisations such as Macra na Feirme youth clubs at county secretary level. She met her husband soon after she started teaching. He had just started up in business on his own in a garage beside the schoolhouse.

'I had tickets to sell and promotions to do. I asked him would he buy a ticket to a dinner dance that was coming up. He said, "Yes, but I've no one to go with". So I said, "Well I have nobody either". So we went along together.

'I was fascinated by the idea of him setting up on his own. I could see that he had a lot of potential, he had a lot of drive and he wanted to get on. I felt, by chatting to him, that I could help to make this a success. As well as this, there was something which immediately gelled between us – we were compatible.'

Rose continued teaching and also became involved in Leo's business. They were married a year later. 'We hadn't a penny. We borrowed money to go on our honeymoon. When we came back we had absolutely nothing to our names. But at least I had a job and he had a £1,000 loan from the banks which he had taken out to set up the business.

'From there we started and I got completely involved with the business. I was teaching by day and in the evenings I'd come home and do the paperwork. Leo worked very hard on the production and manual side of the job, together with his brother Frank, who joined him as an apprentice. It was real teamwork.'

Their son, Enda, was born soon after. 'He was a honeymoon baby. I was still teaching. There was no such thing as maternity leave. I worked right until the end because we couldn't afford otherwise.'

Rose and Leo decided it was time to expand. 'On the birth of our boy, we erected the first part of the factory on a piece of land which we bought beside the house. We had about 100 square feet.' The present-day factory takes up 70,000 square feet.

The couple worked hard, with Rose keeping abreast of all the paperwork as well as teaching in the school. 'I had another baby eighteen months after the first, a girl called Maeve. I taught in a prefab near our house. During my lunch break I'd chase over to the house to say hello to the children. When they were toddling, the two would come over to the school to see me and I'd have to give them a note to take back to the housekeeper saying, "Please don't allow the children to come into the classroom". As soon as school finished, they'd be there to meet me, which was one of the advantages of having the house and the school so close together.'

Business was going well and Leo and Rose decided to concentrate on developing it. Rose shed her dual role. 'In 1976 we called it a day. At that stage it was impossible for me to continue with the school and helping in the business. I was very business orientated. We had already decided that we had to get somebody into the business, so it was decided that I would be the one to go into the business and quit school.

'When Leo went into the bank manager for our annual review and told him what we were doing, he was very concerned that we were losing our only source of regular income.'

Rose did not doubt for a second that it was the right thing to do. 'I was very confident. I never say die until I'm dead. That's my motto. I never give up. If I set out to do something, I'm confident I'm going to achieve it because I won't rest until I do.

'We knew that my husband had the technical expertise. I felt I had the expertise in management and finance, and the drive. So we decided we'd make a go of it. Things changed from that moment on and the business took off year by year and step by step. Frank took over the production side at this stage. Leo went out to meet customers and capture sales.'

There were setbacks, though. 'At one stage, things were not great and we were confined to our local area. Leo said, "Look this isn't going to work", and I said, "No, we've got to make it work, we're not going to give up". I have lots of little mottos up in my office and they inspire me. I have vision. "Give to the world the best you have and the best will come back to you".'

ROSE WAS DETERMINED that her family should not suffer because of the hard work involved in running the company. Her third child, Ciarán, was born in 1978. 'He was reared in the office a lot of the time. The office was so near the home it meant I was never far away and I enjoyed him because I had only one job at this stage. The children knew exactly where I was. I had a side desk in the office where they could come in and sit down to draw or do homework.

'The things that are most important to me in life are my family and my business and both of those are a pleasure and a recreation, so I don't need much else in the line of recreation. I really enjoy my life. I enjoy every day I work. Nothing is a chore to me. And that is the secret of success, really.

'I used to feel guilty. If the children said something to me or were a little bit off, I'd think, "Oh, my God, am I neglecting them?" So, once work is over, I switch straight into children and family. I don't think they've suffered. Our twenty-year-old boy has just finished college and we're very proud of him. Our daughter has gone up today for the results of her college exams. Both are very responsible teenagers.

'We hope some of our children, if not all three, will go into the business,' said Rose, but whether they do or not, she feels that the experience of seeing both parents running a business will stand them in good stead. 'They have much more of an opportunity than other children because they can see the two sides of life in their junior years. They can see me in the role of mother and in my work role. Our daughter was able to type letters when she was ten years old and she can do anything in the company. She can operate the switchboard, type, drive. Both have licences to drive cars. My son has his truck licence and my daughter is taking her test soon.'

Bridging the divide between domestic and work values has brought other advantages, particularly in relations with the staff. 'Way back when we had five or six people, we always tried to treat our staff as family, and even though they've got so numerous now, we still try to keep that human aspect.

'We have very loyal staff and we consider them one of our finest achievements. Some of the people who started with us and were working in the garage are still with us. Very few have left.'

An image that remains in Rose's mind from the early days, when they had 'grave trouble' with the bank, was working through a weekend in order to get the stocktaking done in time for the end-of-year accounts. So that the children could enjoy themselves and not interrupt their parents' work, Leo improvised a seesaw from bits of wood. 'We put it out in the middle of the yard and set the two of them up in the seesaw. And they seesawed away while we counted the stock.

'We really had to prove ourselves before we got the money from the banks in those days. Now we are more stable, thank God.'

The business grew through the quality of the work. 'It grew and grew. At the beginning, it was just Leo and his brother, Frank. They were good, honest workmen and people appreciated that. We have kept that ethos as the firm has grown. It has paid off. People knew we wouldn't con them.'

IN 1976, the Wrights decided to try and sell on the Dublin market, with some trepidation. 'It was a big step. But once we got one customer, we got another – and we still have some of those customers.' Then they decided to move into other areas as well as timber. 'My husband would go off to exhibitions and report back and we'd venture into new fields, such as uPVC windows, accordingly.'

The Leo Wright Group progressed into PVC in 1981 and

then into aluminium. In the last year, the company has started making its own double-glazed units. 'We've covered the full spectrum of the window and door supply market. We mightn't be as cheap as some others, but it has happened that the person who thought we were too expensive went to someone else and the next-door neighbour came back to us. The product was reliable and they realised that a good thing costs a little bit more but is worth it in the long run.'

Rose puts their success down to conscientiousness and attention to detail. She also feels it is vital to enjoy the work and not to let it weigh on you. Here, she feels, women have the edge. 'Even though they say men are tough, I think women are tougher in their outlook and they're able to endure more.'

One impressive example of Rose's resilience and devotion to duty was at the birth of her second son. 'When I was expecting Ciarán I left the office at five o'clock and he was born at five the following morning. I went to Holles Street because I could afford to go to Dublin at this stage. With the others I couldn't. I was four days in Holles Street, but before I left Holles Street I arranged from the phone in the ward for all the cheques to be paid to the suppliers, and as we drove back home with the newborn in the car we picked up about five cheques from customers on the way out of Dublin.'

THE COMPANY HAS never had to advertise, as recommendations have always brought in more work. And the future is bright. 'In latter years we've been looking forward to the European market and we've become more outward-looking. We're now also concentrating on marketing. Our outlook changes as we go on. We have a steady base now so we can do a little bit more in research and development. We go on courses and do a lot of in-house training.'

There are ten women on the staff of 100. 'I try to promote the women in the company because they deserve it. My babysitter is now our main sales co-ordinator. She used to babysit for us when she was fifteen, and after she finished school she joined the company and is with us still.

'I'm beginning now to pick out the good qualities in our staff, not forgetting the women, and develop them so that they can take more responsibility and I can take a back seat. Leo is doing the same. Things tend to weigh him down, whereas I'm more able to cope with pressure. But both of us are looking forward to slowing down a little bit. Other family members have also become involved in the business, including one of my brothers.

'I would like to sit back and take a broader view. When you're working, you are tooth and nail at it. If you relax a little, you can see better. We've been working at setting up a management team for the past few years. The people we are promoting have been with us for a long time and are in tune with the ethos of the company. The attitude of management is very important.'

Rose knows her staff well. Some of them were her pupils at the national school. She makes a point of looking for and bringing out the best in all of them.

DESPITE HER HEAVY WORKLOAD, Rose is still involved in local committees, but has 'no interest whatsoever in politics. I don't vote for parties, I vote for good people and I can pick out good people.

'I am on the committee of the local school so I know what's going on for the children's sakes. I was also involved with the local choir in the church for thirteen years. I love music, singing and dancing. My daughter is very musical and did a lot of Irish dancing. When she was younger I took her to all the Feiseanna round the country. She reached the All-Ireland Irish dancing level. Whatever their interests, I was involved with them.

'Our two sons are now on football teams. I'm a fairly good planner. If I know there's a match on, I'll make sure I'm out of the office and go along to the match and support them. And that's relaxation for me. My family is my hobby. If they're interested in something, I get interested in it too. Ciarán has just started doing moto-cross cycle racing. My husband has taken him for the last two turns, but I'm ready and rearing to go and join in. I would really enjoy that.'

Family holidays are always in Ireland. 'We're not into travelling abroad or into big splashes or show of any kind. We go for the small, simple things in life which are the important things.'

~ *Four* ~

Johanna Saar

President,
Irish Dresden

HOW THE TRADITION OF making fine porcelain transplanted itself from the German town of Thüringen, near Dresden, to Drumcolliher, Co. Limerick, seems properly to belong to a romance novel.

In the late nineteenth century, Anton Müller, a talented young artist, established a workshop in Volkstedt and quickly gained a reputation for his fine lace figurines. He died in 1937 and was succeeded by his son, Herman, also a gifted artist. By the late 1930s, Müller-Volkstedt was well established and was exporting worldwide.

During the Second World War, the factory was completely destroyed. Herman Müller died and his only son was killed on the Eastern front. Johanna Saar, Herman's niece, and her husband, Osker, inherited the ruined factory. Many of the valuable old master moulds were found untouched in the cellars under the ruins.

Johanna and Osker rebuilt the factory in 1945. Just as the business began to flourish, they were forced to leave their home in what was then East Germany. After first setting up in the Black Forest, they moved to Ireland in 1962.

'This year, 1992, is our thirtieth anniversary here,' said Johanna Saar, in a German accent laced with Irish turns of phrase. Aged around seventy, Johanna is youthful, spirited and attractive. She has no intention of retiring.

Before history intervened, Johanna was set to become a doctor. 'I studied medicine. My husband was a pilot in the German airforce during the war. When Osker came home from the war, his profession – a military pilot – was not wanted. Nobody wanted to know. We had to see what we could do.

'I couldn't study any further because by this time we were under Russian occupation. First we were under the Americans, then we were exchanged against a part of Berlin. My husband was taken prisoner by the Russians and was to be transported to Siberia.

'We had already rebuilt the factory with the help of my father and other people. Osker was just about to start making his first sales, the first Americans had arrived, and then the next thing, the Russians marched in and that was the end for us. My husband managed to escape before he was transported to Siberia. He escaped to Western Germany and sent me word to come too, which wasn't so easy because I already had two small children. One was four and the other was just born, she was about two months.

'I made my way across the border. At that time, this was risking your life. I left the children with my mother at first. Then the elder of my children managed to get across with a friend of mine who had a passport saying he could travel between east and west. She travelled as his child. I went on my own. The baby stayed with my mother until much later, and then my sister brought her across.'

Johanna could not afford to be sentimental about leaving her baby. 'I was separated from the baby for a year. She was fine with my mother. In a way, it was much better. We had to build up in Western Germany. We had to see where to live. It was a matter of survival. We were simply glad that my husband hadn't ended up in Siberia.

'If I'd stayed there, I'd also have been in danger of being transported. Things which people think are important today weren't then. We had to have something to eat and try and do something with our lives. Under the Russians, you could be transported for a very little thing. My mother was attacked. This Russian fellow wanted her money and she was attacked on her way to her work, helping my father in his timber business. Another neighbour of mine was killed for a bottle of brandy.

'They were bad times. My sister and myself were locked away in the presses when the evening came because those soldiers were searching the houses for women, and other things. That is the way it was in those days. They were dangerous times.

'So we ended up in West Germany and we started to build another factory. We stayed for ten years and we had it quite well on the go. We were exporting to other countries, to America and so on. This was in the 1950s. Germany became very industrialised. This is when the wonders happened. We had to import foreign labour, and labour was very expensive. My factory is very labour intensive. Everything is done by hand. So that is why we were looking elsewhere. We couldn't get people to work for us. If we could, it was too expensive.'

The Irish connection came when they met a man from Roscrea at a trade fare. He was in the building trade and was promoting investment in Ireland. He brought them to Drumcolliher where there was a development association in place to encourage industry. 'I am often asked, "Why Drumcolliher?" I don't know. We just arrived and that was it.

'I knew nothing at all about Ireland. I knew there was Dublin and that was all. It was totally unimportant in our geography lessons in school. We would just have learned it was the last stop before America. I don't remember anyone talking about Ireland much before the war. Maybe it was too difficult to come here.'

Thinking of her school days brings back painful memories for Johanna. 'When the war came in Germany, I was in my last year at school. I was doing my Abitur. The boys from my class went straight to the war. Four weeks later, some were dead, another one had no legs. Young people of eighteen years of age. What for?'

JOHANNA WAS less than impressed with Drumcolliher, a tiny village which even today has few amenities. The Germany she had left behind was fast becoming synonymous with progress. 'When we first came here, I didn't want to stay here because I just didn't like it one bit. Coming from Germany, ending up in Drumcolliher thirty years ago ... it was dreadful. I thought it was the end of my life.

'By now I had four children. When I saw the house we were supposed to live in I said we couldn't live there. It was

a big farmhouse. It was very nice to look at but it was difficult to live in because of the cold in the winter. I was not
used to the climate at all. I got very ill then. I didn't want to
invest anything here. I only wanted to go home. The sooner
the better.'

She remembers with horror trying to buy meat in those
early days. 'Even if you wanted to buy something here, you
couldn't. The butcher shop had halves of animals hanging
up and if you wanted a bit they'd just take a saw to it. Then
you got the piece packed into newspaper with string around
it.'

Osker, on the other hand, was captivated. 'My husband
loved it from the first minute. We all spoke school English,
so that helped. I'm used to it now. Then I had no choice. I
don't think I would have stayed here if I had. But there was
no going back because my real home was in Eastern Germany. I had to make it work and that's all there was to it.
That's the way I look at things anyway. You just have to
make things work if you want to get anywhere.'

The main difficulty in getting the business started was
training people with no tradition in the craft to make the
fine porcelain figurines. 'We had made ourselves a five-year
plan to get this thing off the ground, but it didn't work. Our
merchandise after five years was still far away from being
good enough to be offered on the world market.' Neverthe-
less, Johanna went to America to show the company's
wares. The reaction was not favourable.

'People here were not used to any kind of work, except
occasional agricultural or building work. Nobody had seen
a piece of porcelain like this. In Germany it takes three
years' training for people to reach the required standard.
But they have a tradition of doing it in Germany. Here, they
had to start from scratch.'

Johanna brought people over from Germany to help train
the local people. Her biggest setback on the training front
was when she paid for five of her staff to go over and train
in Germany. 'None of them came back. They just loved it in
Germany. Life was better. They could earn good money

over there. We had spent all this time and money training them and we were back to square one. It was dreadful.' As always when she says something was dreadful, Johanna breaks into laughter.

It took ten years, rather than the estimated five, for Johanna to be in any way ready to take on the international market. 'After five years, we were ready to a certain extent. We made things and we sold them, but we had no impact on the outside market. We sold to the tourists. At this time the Americans would buy anything. It took ten years really before we were in full swing and that is far too long.'

To make ends meet they made objects which would probably have made the Müllers turn in their graves. 'It's not that we had nothing to offer. We made leprechauns at the time and little donkeys – to train the people, to get them into the mood. And then later on we made the finer things. They were sold in Ireland. It was the only way, though at the time there were many small crafts shops in Ireland that sold to the tourists.'

Johanna still has people working for her who started with the company in the 1960s. 'They liked the work. It is important to this industry that people stay because it is so difficult to learn the process.'

FIVE YEARS after Osker and Johanna moved to Ireland, Osker died of a heart attack. 'Then I thought the best thing is that I die as well. Things were very bad in that year. I thought I'd buy myself a coffin too. The man who brought us over here was a great help, as were other men in the area who had been friends of my husband. I also got some help from official sources like Shannon Development And I was able to borrow some money. The bank manager felt sorry for me, I think.

'We carried on. We lived from week to week trying to get the wages money ready and so on. From there on we developed. I went back to America with a better collection this time. In the early 1970s, I made a few friends in the business, people my uncle had sold to when I was a child. I showed them the collection and they gave me some good advice. That was the breakthrough in the American market.'

The name Irish Dresden was adopted to appeal to the American market. The company now employs 50 people, of whom four are men. Its main exports are to America and Japan and they also export to England, France and Sweden. They have the elegant White Gold shop in Limerick and a shop in Adare.

'We have our own office in Japan to explore the Japanese market. We also have our own distribution there. We're very well known in Japan. We have a name. The Japanese buy the name more than the product as such.'

Irish Dresden bring out a new collection every year. The figurine that made them famous was Sinéad, a young girl in a long flounced lace dress, who sits playing the harp. She is still one of their best-selling figurines.

JOHANNA RUNS the company with her eldest daughter, Sabina, who is the production manager. Her other three daughters have also been involved in the company at one time or another. Corry used to be the marketing manager and was based in the Japan office for a couple of years. Angelika used to run the shop in Adare. Susie used to run the White Gold shop and is now living in Australia with her second husband.

'All my daughters have married twice,' says Johanna, slightly bemused. 'I have lots of sons-in-law.'

Johanna does not plan to expand the company greatly: 'As long as I am here, I think we'll stay about the size we are.' But neither has she any intention of putting her feet up. 'I think this is very boring. I don't think I would stay here then. What am I doing in Drumcolliher if I'm not working? It's not for me. If you don't have your health, this is different.

'I hate retired people, they have an ache here and and an ache there. You get sick if you're thinking every day and you have no other interests.'

Johanna's business and social life tend to overlap. Many of her friends are also her customers and she has long-held connections with porcelain buyers in several countries.

She often works long hours late at night, 'Not because I have to, but because I like it.'

JOHANNA IS philosophical about work and does not hanker after the career she originally trained for. 'I was a doctor in the early days because that was the profession I had chosen. But at the end of the day, if you like your work and you have success, it makes no difference what you do. The past is history. If things don't work out and you spend your time moaning and crying about it, you get nowhere. There's no point. There's something nice in everything you do. You just have to see the beauty.

'That goes for the country I found myself in as well. If I didn't see any beauty in Ireland, it would have been awful. Germany has changed so much since I left that maybe I wouldn't like it at all if I lived there now.'

When the wall came down in 1989, Johanna went back to Berlin with her sister. 'I remembered this beautiful house with landscaped gardens and a tree-lined avenue. When I got there I was horrified. The gardens had disappeared, the trees had been destroyed. The house had the windows hanging off it. There were five families living there. It was heartbreaking to see what had become of it.

'It's the same for the whole of Eastern Germany, it's totally run down. The premises of my father's timber company is now a factory making shabby furniture. My father left for West Germany in 1953. He couldn't stay either. If you had possessions at that time you were in danger. They would transport you God knows where, you would never be seen again. Those who could, left.

'People I spoke to who had stayed really suffered a lot during those forty years. They couldn't do anything. One friend said he couldn't even paint his house because he would have been accused of having connections with the western world, even of being a spy.

'I think it will take ten years to rebuild Eastern Germany. Every house is run down. There are now flats where the little factory was that we rebuilt after the war. The old kiln which we had at the time is still there. You can't use it any more and it should have been got rid of, but it's still standing there the way we left it.

'It was very emotional going back. I plan to take my children before it all changes. When I went over, you could still see the border line where so many people were shot. We were lucky. We made it.'

AT THE END OF THE DAY, Johanna is glad that the factory ended up in Ireland. The cross-fertilisation of a German tradition and an Irish location has resulted in a unique product.

'I don't think we did so badly here. The name of Irish Dresden represents something very special. When we first started selling in America, nobody believed that the figurines were made in Ireland. That was why the name was invented and lots of promotion was done to say they were crafted by Irish people. I said, "Why in the name of God should Irish people not be able to do this? They do lovely knitting. They have good hands and they are artistic".

'We have found a lot of talent in this village. We did not think it at first, but it was here all around us. Today we are selling better than rival factories in Germany.'

~ *Five* ~

Angela Collins O'Mahoney

Managing Director,
Collins Steeplejacks

ANGELA COLLINS O'MAHONEY formed Collins Steeple-jacks in her home village, Kilkishen, Co. Clare, in 1966. Three years later, the company was contracted by Electronic Space Systems Corporation of Boston to carry out a job at Shannon airport. They were to erect a radome, a giant structure used to protect radar equipment.

Not only did Angela's company complete the contract satisfactorily, but she also convinced the Americans to build a factory in Kilkishen to manufacture the radomes. A joint company, Essco Collins Ltd, was created in 1974.

Angela's husband, John, left his job as a member of the garda síochána and joined the firm. Their employees travelled from Kilkishen to install radomes all over the world, including Bulgaria, Romania and Guadeloupe.

Meanwhile, Angela was jetting around the world on sales trips – to Nigeria, Moscow, Kenya and Rio de Janeiro. In 1979, she travelled with the Irish Export Board (Córas Tráchtála) to China where she won a large contract. The company in Kilkishen doubled in size. Production of new products began. Soon they were manufacturing antenna systems for satellite communications and radio astronomy.

In 1985, the company won a further £2.5 million order from China and had to extend its premises again. It seemed that everything she touched turned to gold. In 1986, Minister Bruton presented her with the Bowmaker Award for Irish Industry.

YET Angela was never comfortable with the image of a jet-setting industrialist. Her heart was at home, with a family that embraced foster children, aunts and grandparents. Angela has three daughters, now aged twenty-three, fourteen, and seven and a son aged twenty. She fostered her youngest daughter when she was two weeks old, and later adopted her.

Angela remembers how a certain Mrs Howard came to join the family: 'When my son was one week old, I was living in a new neighbourhood in a new house. My husband was in China. A woman greeted me and said, "Welcome to the parish". I asked her to come in and see the baby, and she came in and stayed for seventeen years.

'I moved house from that place about five years later and she came with me and lived with us till she died. She had nobody belonging to her and she was gorgeous. She was about ninety when she died. My mother and my dad also lived with us so we had three old people. Then John's sisters came to live with us. As one would marry out of the house, another would come. He was the eldest of eight.'

Angela was the youngest in her family. She had four brothers. 'I think that was a good thing in the younger years. They toughened me up. I had to fight to survive. They'd be the first at the table.'

She was born in Kilkishen, Co. Clare, near Shannon. 'I lived on a little farm with my parents. I got a very modest education. We didn't have much money. My dad drank a lot. He was in debt. But we got loads and loads of love. Even though they didn't come across as loving each other, they poured the love into us. That gave us great confidence when we grew up.

'I left school at about sixteen and I went to the city, Limerick, to do a commercial course. I realised the hardship on my mother to keep me at school and I wanted to go out and get a job and produce some money. I felt all the other girls were going down town spotting the fellas but I wouldn't. I felt I had to get on with my learning, so I'd practise on the typewriter during dinner hours. I wanted to make my mother proud. We were very close. Then I got a job at seventeen. The teacher was very good to me and she gave me the first job that came along, knowing the circumstances.'

Angela went to work for a steeplejack company in 1966. She worked in the office and would also climb to heights of 500 feet. 'A woman hardly worked outside the home, let alone as a steeplejack. Mr Lynch would send me out to sites to deliver materials. If it was a site in Dublin, I could be beeping my hooter at the bottom of the chimney and these fellas would pay no heed to me. And I'd be wanting to get back to Limerick so I'd climb up the thing and say, "I've been down here for half an hour and you didn't see me". They'd say, "If we were to come down every time we heard a horn blowing we'd be up and down all day". So that's how I learned to climb. I was not afraid at all.'

There was an engineering shop at the rear of the offices and she would also experiment with welding and grinding equipment. When her employer died, the company was dormant. Angela decided to start her own company. 'While my employer was alive, I never knew my strengths. I never took any heed of the work I was doing.'

SOON AFTER Angela started up the business, she had a major break. 'I was about two years married and I was expecting Susan, my eldest, when Gay Byrne's office phoned me. I think RTE was only two or three years old and there was only one channel. I was asked to go on the programme. I was so shocked I thought somebody was having a joke. They wanted to interview me. I climbed up to the top of a church, six months pregnant, and they filmed me. On the same show were Phyllis Diller the comedian and Stanley Baker, she remembers.

It was around this time that the American company, Essco, were looking for a firm to erect the radome at Shannon Airport. A representative of the company contacted Angela having heard of her television exploits.

'The American got in touch with me and we started work. We did it so fast, we were like little leprechauns and very excited about working for an American. I figured that if we worked very well, listened to him, we might get to do this in other countries. So he went back to the States very impressed with us and he said that his boss would come over and talk to us.

'The following year, the president of his company came over to see us. He was lovely and he came along with his family. We told him that we'd love to go round and erect these things all over the world. I was looking at the map and I was thinking "Where's Cyprus, where are these places?" He said he'd employ us. We ended up working for them all over the world, you name it, Nigeria, Mexico. This was around 1974.'

Angela then saw another opportunity. She suggested to the president of the company that he set up a factory to make the radomes in Ireland. At the time, they were being made in England. She explained that he would receive a grant from the Irish government to build the factory, and training grants for the men they needed to employ. She also offered to give him the site for the factory in return for a partnership in the venture. 'We formed a joint venture, Essco Collins, the head office was in America, sales office in England and the main manufacturer in Kilkishen, Co. Clare.

'All the technology was transferred to the village. Now, when the village people heard of it they couldn't believe there was going to be a factory built. You couldn't even get up the road for the trees meeting on top. It was fourteen miles from Shannon. There wasn't even water. At the opening of the factory, which is now eighteen years ago, the minister who opened it had to climb over the bonnet of his car to get into the place. But it grew fast. It was unbelievable.'

Angela appeared on The Late Late Show again in 1982. 'I loved going on the television for the publicity but I was terrified. A woman in business at that time was so rare that if I only walked sideways there was television coverage. I had all the magazines after me and appeared in a book about the top ten Irish companies. In 1985, I climbed to the top of the County Hall in Cork in a race organised for the "Cork 800" celebrations. I won it, which led to more publicity.'

By 1984, Angela had 40 men working for her. The company, which she had originally started from her own home, grew from a turnover of £75 a week to £1.5 million a year. The busier she became, however, the more she regretted not being at home with her family.

'We had 27% shares in the company, for putting up the four acres of land for the site and about £11,000; it was mostly American-owned. It took three months to build the factory. Then, for ten years I was travelling the world. I'm in a suitcase and I'm in the Hiltons and the Concordes and so is John, my husband. We're saluting each other in the sky.

'And I'm all the time thinking about my background. My mother was always there when I used to go in and if she wasn't there it was like a mortuary. And I'd always think "Oh, my kids, my babies". They had the other members of the family around. I was the one who felt the loss, they did not. They were lovely kids, they were not spoilt or cheeky. I think it was because they had so many old people around them.

'When I'd come home at the weekend, I'd see this old woman, Mrs Howard; my son would fall and he'd run to her and I'd feel as if it was a knife through me. Ten years, and the first two are nearly grown up. We had this other little one who's now fifteen. I said, "I'm going to get rid of the plane and I'm going to get rid of the high life". Mind you, I always felt out of my depth. I only did it purely for the money, and because the opportunity was there.

'We had all these men employed and the men loved to go all over the world, I mean how could you stop? They were in Jamaica, China.'

IN 1984, Angela had several setbacks with her health. She had to have a hysterectomy and cysts removed and had to cope with the onset of the menopause. 'I was a year and three months knocked out. This took a little bit of my confidence away. I was sort of depressed and everything.

'I think they blew it out of all kind of proportion on the medical side of things. They said I was going to get flabby very fast and get hair and all sorts of things. I thought I was going to turn into a bear! I didn't have time to read up on these things and understand my body and understand myself, so I was waiting for all these things to happen, and nothing was happening.'

For health reasons and in order to spend more time with her family, Angela decided to retreat from work a little. 'Money wasn't everything now. We had more money than we could cope with. We decided to move in other directions.'

She decided to sell the shares in Essco and buy Landscape House which had 34 rooms and was set in 63 acres of land surrounded by the River Shannon near Doonass, Co. Clare. 'It hadn't been lived in since 1953. There were calves in the hall and grass growing everywhere. We decided we'd take on this derelict house and turn it into a leisure centre.

'I was still running Collins Steeplejacks, and was doing some work for Essco Collins but the Americans were really running the company. I was arranging grants, coming to Dublin to the embassies and trying to sell. It was a glamorous position. I would meet the Americans when they came over and show them around and introduce them to this minister and that minister. I was able to continue doing that and start work on the house. I hung 480 rolls of wallpaper and painted everywhere.

'I got £100,000 for my shares. They didn't want us to sell our shares, but I thought one in the hand is better than two in the bush. Things were beginning to look bad for business generally, people were closing all around.'

IT TOOK fourteen years to restore the house to its original condition. 'In the first year we made it habitable and then went on to extend the out-offices and make them into chalets.'

Angela and her husband formed Landscape Game and Leisure Centre in 1985. Further down the river, a pub had come up for sale. They also bought and developed this.

Eventually they made a total break from Essco-Collins.

'We finally resigned from Essco Collins, my husband and I. The managers had been there eighteen years and were now doing well. At the beginning, they needed us and the money we put in. We worked for nothing and nurtured the company but now it was standing on its own feet and the Americans had all the influence. The work was not being distributed evenly and my workers tended to be sent to the less popular places where weather conditions were bad and it was hard to get the work finished on time.

'My thanks is to see the factory there and all the people employed. To see a factory in your own town, which had nothing, is a tremendous achievement. Now Kilkishen is not a village any more. It's a town. There are houses everywhere.

'In a way, I regret selling the shares because I could have retained some influence in the company. But my whole pattern is: create, see that the thing is up and running and leave.'

ANGELA'S NEXT PROJECT was to build a golf course in the grounds of the leisure centre. Seven years later, she decided to sell it. 'I had a factory where I came from and a golf course where I came to live.'

Angela still manages Collins Steeplejacks but is now concentrating more on home life. 'We now have a stud farm on 38 acres. The house is a ranch. We moved here two years ago. My dream now is to make the house as I want it. I have lots of ideas and enjoy interior decoration. And I want to be a good mother to the two children still at home.

'I'd love to cook a dinner for my children and for them to depend on me when they come in to have a meal ready. Maybe it's only for a year but I'd love to be a wife. Now I am looking for a rest. I want to look back and try to reflect. My guilt came through all those years of not being there so I'm going to try being there for a little while.'

Despite her current yearning for domesticity, Angela Collins O'Mahoney has no regrets about her achievements. 'It was a great success from having nothing, and we really had nothing.'

She feels women are generally capable of a lot more than they think. 'I would like to encourage women who haven't been educated and who have come from a modest background not to wait for a crisis to find their strength but to look at themselves and see what they are capable of doing. And at the end of the day I would say to them not to forget their family, because if you don't bring up your family well then you lose everything.'

~ *Six* ~

Eileen O'Mara Walsh

**Managing Director, O'Mara Travel
Director, Great Southern Hotel Group**

EILEEN O'MARA WALSH was first appointed chairperson of the board of Great Southern Hotels in 1984, and was re-appointed by two successive governments. She was largely responsible for turning a loss-making, run-down chain of hotels into a highly profitable enterprise. She also runs her own successful travel agency, which has the Club Mediter-ranean franchise for Ireland, and she is the founder of the Irish Tourism Industry Federation.

Despite her much publicised association with Great Southern Hotels, she would not like to be known primarily for her work with the group. 'It's certainly one of the great achievements in my career, but really I'd like to be known as someone who has achieved a fairly modest success in my own business and who has had a fair degree of influence in the broad tourist industry.

'I've been heavily involved for ten years in the general policy and lobbying process of the tourist industry. There's a certain degree of politics with a small "p" in it. You're in-volved on a national level. I wouldn't be interested in poli-tics with a capital "P". I wouldn't like to be exposed that much, or to be on call all the time. I don't know how poli-ticians do it. They are such prisoners of their constituencies. You could have no time for private life. Whereas you can involve yourself in business, even on a national level, and still have a fairly low profile.'

Eileen does not actively seek publicity. 'Having got to this stage, I've accepted a modest profile, but I'm uncom-fortable with coverage. It may be a female trait. In fact, the reason I respond positively to things like interviews is be-cause I feel it's important for women to be seen to be suc-cessful in business.

'It's important to stand up and be counted. I spoke re-cently at a symposium on equal opportunities for women and that was one of the things that came out. It's very im-portant to have role models, particularly in business. At the

Irish Management Institute conference, for example, you see the audience sitting there in serried rows of business suits. Even though women are coming along, they are still very much the exception.

'There are certain women who have been identified and the media tend to come back to them again and again, whereas I do think there's another stratum of women who are running small businesses. It seems to be very hard for women to break through in structured organisations. In small businesses you don't have those hierarchies to work through. Women also tend to do well in people industries like advertising, travel, tourism, show business, and journalism.'

EILEEN HAS BEEN involved in the hotel and travel business since she left school. Her first job was as a chambermaid in London.

'I left school in 1959, aged eighteen, with the Leaving Certificate. My family were not well off and I simply had to find a job. I wanted to go abroad. It was the usual thing at the time to get out of Ireland, quite unlike now when everyone wants to stay in Ireland. The only way I could get my parents to agree to my going to London was if I got a live-in job, so I got a job as a chambermaid in the Grosvenor House Hotel.

'I think I lasted six weeks. Domesticity was never my strong point. I then got a job as a management trainee, or general dogsbody, in the White House Hotel Group where I had a variety of duties, including receptionist and restaurant cashier.'

Eileen stayed with the group for two years and then went to Paris. 'The whole French influence has been a strong element in my career.' When she returned to Ireland she worked in the French Embassy and the Alliance Française for a while. Then her first first job in tourism came up.

'Bord Fáilte opened an office in Paris in 1967, their first

office. I got the job as their first "travel adviser", giving people information about going to Ireland. I was about twenty-four or twenty-five at the time. It was a breakthrough. A good job, with a good salary in a good organisation with good possibilities. In addition, I was getting to know the Irish tourism product.

'I didn't last all that long. I came back over here for personal reasons after eighteen months – I was madly in love with an Irish painter.' There were other contributing factors. 'Even though I liked working in Paris and I liked Bord Fáilte, I realised that to move from being a mere travel adviser to something with more responsibility would have been difficult in such a large organisation.

'So I came back here and got a job with USIT, Union of Students in Ireland Travel. It is still going strong but was in early days then. It was a very progressive, adventurous travel company involved in setting up student charter flights all over the world. There was a great international network of student travel companies who were partially owned by the union and partly private. It was a very entrepreneurial, very young company.'

Eileen set up their tours department. She had to think up tour themes for student visitors to Ireland. 'I set up things like horse-drawn caravan holidays, bicycling holidays and cultural tours. I loved doing that.'

The company expanded into commercial as well as student travel and set up Blue Skies and Stephen's Green Travel. 'I moved within the company to a couple of different divisions and ended up being manager of Stephen's Green Travel. I was about thirty at that time. I probably would have stayed. I don't think I had any great impetus to start my own business. As always in these things, accident came into play, or chance or opportunity.'

The company broke up. The commercial end of it was sold off, management was made redundant and Eileen could have walked away with £5,000. 'That was the moment of truth, I suppose. At that stage I had a two-year-old child. I wasn't married. This was was quite an issue in the mid-

1970s, though not with USIT, which, with its roots in youth travel, was fairly forward-looking.

'I sat down and thought about it. I said to myself, "Do I really want to go out and find another job?" I'd still be working for somebody else, I'd still be bound to the nine to five.

'There was a division within the company that was being sold off, the tourist division. I'd set it up, I enjoyed the work involved, I knew everybody. All the contacts abroad were my contacts. So I decided that instead of taking redundancy I would ask to take over the goodwill of that company.

'The company agreed. I was able to sublet an upstairs office at Stephen's Green and I set up O'Mara Travel.

'I felt great. It was a risk of course, but I've always been inclined to take risks, in a certain way. I don't take many financial risks, but I take a certain amount of risk in decision-making. I must say it was the best thing I ever did and I've never really looked back.

'There have been a lot of problems. Business isn't easy. But at least I didn't have to answer to anybody else. I probably put in more hours, but some of the hours I could put in at home. If I was stuck I could bring a carrycot into the office. It was *my* office, so to hell with anybody who objected.'

WHEN HER SON, Eoin, was a baby and Eileen was still working for USIT, she found child minders were often a source of worry. 'I had a great child minder who was passed on to me by a friend. She had four kids and she was a very practical Dublin woman. One day when Eoin was eighteen months old, I went to see her. I had been trying to sort out my taxes. I wasn't earning much and I found that I could get some sort of relief if I claimed that I was paying somebody to mind my child. I don't know what it was exactly but I know that it was very small. The child minder didn't want to be declared so I had put down that I was paying her half of what I was actually paying her so that she wouldn't come

into the tax net. I explained this to her and went home with
Eoin.

'That night a letter was slipped through the letter box
saying "Don't bring Eoin tomorrow morning, my husband
won't have anything to do with tax". End of story. So I had
work the next morning and nowhere to leave the child. He
was very attached to her and I thought she was to him.'

Eileen feels that major policy changes need to be implemented by the Government with regard to the whole business of child minding.

THE O'MARAS have a family history of running businesses.
Eileen's father was not himself directly involved in starting
a business, but her grandfather was.

'Way back, my grandfather was a well-known opera
singer. His fame hasn't really lasted because it was before
the era of recordings. He died in 1928, so I never knew him.
He had the O'Mara Opera Company. The family business in
Limerick was the O'Mara Bacon Company, so I decided I'd
continue the tradition and have the O'Mara Travel Company.

Eileen was the youngest of three girls. Her sisters are six
and eight years older. 'When I was starting out in business,
one of my sisters was in the theatre and the other was working in London in the BBC. We were all quite independent
and did our own thing.

'I was brought up to feel I had to be economically independent. My father didn't do well. He was one of these
people who try things and sometimes they work. He started
out quite well off with a good business and ended up poorly
off.

'My mother would probably be the strongest force and I
think I found that because she worried so much about
making ends meet, I didn't want to be in that position. She
didn't work. She was an English liberal and socialist and
very strong-minded. She met my father in England before

the war and they moved back here after war broke out. I was born here during the war. One of my sisters, who works with me now, remembers being sent over here on a boat with a label round her neck and a gas mask.

'My father had emigrated from Ireland in the 1920s. There's always a bit of a veil put over this, but he was slightly involved in the War of Independence. The family didn't approve and he was shipped off to Canada. I think he had been wounded, he'd got into trouble anyway. He spent twenty years abroad living in England and Canada and only came back here and joined the family business during the war.'

THE GREAT SOUTHERN HOTEL connection came through Eileen's involvement in the travel business generally. 'My company was not huge, in fact it was very modest in those days, just myself and somebody else working part-time. I got the Club Med account by simply going and asking for it. I spoke French and they had a connection with the company I used to work for.'

Yet the extent of her involvement in the travel business as a whole was greater than the size of her company would indicate. 'I somehow or other was always involved in committees. For example, agents at that time involved in the inbound business had an association. I suppose if you're vocal and articulate you get elected onto committees and you suddenly find yourself running the thing.

'In the early 1980s, I was involved in the National Tourism Council. It was pretty ineffective. In fact, I was elected president of it. I could see it wasn't going anywhere. Like a lot of women I'm quite practical and I don't like being involved in things unless I can see that I can put a shape on them, and that they mean something.

'I suggested to a number of people, who were much more senior in tourism than I was, that we should reshape it, that we needed a national organisation to represent the tourist industry. The senior people, the head of Bord Fáilte at the time and the head of Aer Lingus, listened to me. Things were going badly for tourism then. VAT was high and we weren't getting anywhere with Government. It was a Cinderella industry, nobody really cared about it.

'The powers that be were receptive to my suggestions. I wasn't allied to any of the big guns. I wasn't a state company. I was probably seen as a good, objective, non-aligned, independent person in the industry. So I founded the Irish Tourist Industry Confederation, which is the CII (Confederation of Irish Industry) of tourism. All the big companies were involved. The trick was really to get the chief executives to join so it wouldn't be passed down the line where no decisions could be taken.'

The chief executives duly joined and formed a council and Eileen was its first chairperson. 'The council had quite a high profile and consequently so did I. In 1984, the then president of Labour, Ruairí Quinn, got in touch with me. He had had Great Southern Hotels thrust upon him, I suppose. They used to belong to CIE, the state transport company. They'd been losing £1 million a year, being at the tail end of a transport company which had no money anyway.

'There was great talk at the time about selling them off. There was disagreement in cabinet, however, so it was decided not to sell them but to hive them off as an independent company, still owned by the State but with their own board of management.

'I was asked by Ruairí Quinn to become a director first of all. I had never been asked to be a director of a state company before but I said, "Why not?" Then he asked me to become chairman and that was a bigger decision. I asked a couple of people's advice and their reaction was that I would be taking on too much and that my own business would suffer.

'But I felt at the back of it there was the implication that it was too difficult for a woman, so I thought "To hell with it, I'll do it". I was chairman for seven years. I was reappointed by Bertie Ahern. I was actually appointed to state companies by Labour, Fine Gael and Fine Fáil.'

There were large budgets involved but Eileen was undaunted. 'Looking back, you learn an awful lot as you go along. Fools rush in where angels fear to tread. I had an instinct that it would be all right. I knew the industry and I knew the hotel from being a supplier. I would put groups into those hotels and I knew how run down they were. I also knew what they could be. I might have been more scared about it had I thought about the implications more. On the other hand, I'm inclined to take an opportunity if it comes along.'

Eileen also felt, looking around at the other directors, that there really was nobody better placed than she was to carry out the work involved. There was also a rescue package attached. 'I wouldn't have taken on the hotels, I don't think anybody in business would have, unless there was a rescue package. The old debts were going to be written off, and money was going to be put in. That was the key to bringing them back on the road to profitability. They turned around within three years from being £1 million down to breaking even. Last year they made £2 million profit.

'We never had any other cash injection from the State since the initial one in 1984. They paid off the debts and they put £3 million into doing them up a bit. From then on, we relied on profits and ordinary commercial borrowings.'

The Great Southern Hotel group has now been bought by Aer Rianta. Eileen is a director on the new board. 'The idea now is to expand, possibly into Dublin and Cork, possibly into the UK. I'm less involved on a day-to-day basis than I was and am consequently putting more into O'Mara Travel. I'm still involved in the Tourist Industry Confederation as a council member and I'm director now of the Medieval Trust which I'm very keen on.'

EILEEN DESCRIBES O'Mara Travel as a medium-sized business. 'Our inbound business, tourism, is one distinct section of it and we bring in about 5,000 people. Our outbound business, which is Club Med, is another section, and sends out about 2,000 people a year.'

When she herself goes on holiday, she admits, she is inclined to go to the west of Ireland. 'The greatest luxury for me now is time. What I'd really like to do is take a month and travel by train and take a villa somewhere in Italy and just do nothing.'

Eileen sometimes visits Eoin's father's family in Westport: 'It's a real West of Ireland sprawling family with all the interconnections of cousins and aunts and uncles. There are millions of them.' Eileen appreciates dipping into family life and sees roots and security as vital, especially as she grows older.

At the same time, she values being single and enjoys the camaraderie she has with her son, who is now sixteen. She finds it relaxing to come home in the evening and just talk about something like football with him. 'It switches you off from your business and you don't have to worry whether your partner's had a bad day at work, for example, or had a row with his boss.'

While marriage wasn't very important for Eileen, having a child was. 'You never look back. It was a breakthrough having Eoin. Before having him, I lived in a rented flat. I couldn't have cared less about property or business or anything really. The realisation that I had a child to care for pushed me into buying a house and starting a business. In fact, Eoin laughs about this and says I didn't get anywhere until he came along.'

EILEEN CONSIDERS that women are late developers. 'I honestly think that women don't start developing until they're thirty. Women in their twenties are scurrying around the place honed in still on this nesting and emotional thing.'

'I'm fifty now. I found that very difficult to come to terms with. I didn't mind being thirty, I didn't mind being forty, but I really hated being fifty. It was nothing to do with ageing as such, it was more to do with career. I suddenly felt that's it. Whatever I've done, that's it.'

It is doubtful whether this is the case. Eileen O'Mara Walsh certainly has the energy and enthusiasm to carry out a few more projects yet. Not only is her business flourishing, but she is also an active art collector. Looking back on her career, she is surprised that it didn't revolve around the visual arts.

'Art is a great interest. If I have an odd few bob it goes on paintings. Throughout the Swinging Sixties, I was very much involved with the arts and thought that was where my career would have been. I'm not creative myself, though I would like to write at some stage, but certainly I'm a collector.' She ponders for a while and adds, 'You never know, perhaps my second career will be writing.'

~ *Seven* ~

Marna Fleming

Managing Director,
Trista's Ltd

TRISTA'S, a food company based in Dundalk which specialises in flavoured mayonnaise, started when Marna Fleming made too much mayonnaise for a local country market. Now established for five years, Trista's has its own distribution network all over Ireland, and supplies Marks and Spencer in France.

Marna Fleming has an abundance of energy which was not contained by running a home and bringing up four young children. A trained nurse, a profession she loved, she was forced to leave because of the marriage bar. Having gone off at several tangents, she set up Trista's with her husband, Michael, who has a science background.

Marna's personality is the main impetus behind the company. Her 'rushes of adrenalin', she acknowledges, are the driving force. Making mayonnaise was the fourth business idea she followed up, having achieved a degree of success with the others.

MARNA MARRIED just days before the lifting of the marriage ban, which prohibited married women from working in the public sector. 'I handed in my notice and went off on honeymoon and three days later the marriage ban had been lifted.'

'I was quite happy at home,' Marna continued. 'We live up the side of a mountain. It's a beautiful, tranquil setting. I had three kids very quickly so they took up a lot of my time. I would also read a lot and enjoyed walking. But you can only read so much and you can only walk so much. I always had a lot of hobbies, and some of these gradually evolved into business ideas.'

Marna thanks her erratic childhood for her range of interests and her business instinct. 'I had an erratic upbringing which enables me now to cope with crises. My husband was brought up to believe life has to be orderly. I was brought up to believe there'd be an odd spate of orderliness but mostly there'd be a crisis.

'My mother was very artistic and my father read a lot. There were three brothers and myself in the family and we had a family business, a pub and grocery. It went from being very successful and very lucrative to going through extremely bad years from the time I was eleven, primarily because Dundalk went into a major industrial crisis. We all had to chip in and work. There was a lot of stress in my parents' relationship.

'We got on all right with them separately and years later when we all left home and saw that our parents were doing extremely well without us, we realised that maybe they shouldn't have had us in the first place. We were a lot of stress when money was very bad. There was a lot I knew about life not being perfect, and I think that's positive. There's a lot of fun as well in situations like that, which a lot of families miss out on – fun and colour, happy memories.'

AFTER SHE LEFT nursing, Marna's first enterprise was to make souvenirs. 'Between Waterford Glass and Beleek there's not much available in Ireland in the way of decent souvenirs. There is nothing that really expresses the culture and mythology of the country.

'I saw an ad in a magazine, this is going back eighteen or nineteen years, for a company in Hull, England, that did prototypes of moulds if you did the designs. The man I spoke to on the phone was amused by me, I think he thought I was quite eccentric. I did various designs and posted them over. The one that took off was for an Irish crib scene. It was a beautiful Celtic crib with men in Aran sweaters and fish in a basket. The kings were in the style of the mythical Cúchullain.

'I would fill the moulds with lead-weighted plaster and then I hand-painted them. I made hundreds of the things and people bought them. They sold through word of mouth. People would say, "What'll I give you for that?" And I would say, "I haven't a clue", because I enjoyed doing it.'

Marna's husband, Michael, generally resists a little when she first has an idea, then he comes round and tries to help, though not always successfully.

'I used to paint all night, literally, when the kids had gone to bed. It was really peaceful. Michael would already have made the moulded figures for me.

'Quite often, though, the moulds would run out and I'd be shouting for him to make some more. One night I was out with some friends and Michael thought to himself, "I'll fix this one – she won't be coming to me and saying, 'Where's me moulds?'"

'He made a big bucket of the stuff and had the moulds all lined up. But as he went to pour the plaster out he realised it had set solid in the bucket. He'd forgotten how fast drying it was. He debated whether he should throw it over a wall somewhere into a field so that I'd never know.'

MARNA'S FOUR CHILDREN are called Torin, Syro, Trista and Dagan. 'Torin was my eldest child. I'm not that heavy into religion and I wanted something that sounded nice but wasn't terribly Catholic.' Torin would watch Marna paint the figures and she used to let him paint any of the failures.

One day he asked her what name she was going to sell them under. I hadn't thought of calling them anything, but I went along with him. I bought some labels and I hand-wrote in an old sienna ink "Torin Crafts" and put a little flower inside the label.'

As the models were proving successful, Marna decided to approach the Arts Council of Ireland. 'I'll always remember the grouchy ex-army type who greeted me. He said they didn't give out feasibility studies or grants for Irish crafts because it's a proven industry. I was in with him for two-and-a-half hours. At the end of two hours, he said, "Jesus, you can have a grant. You've me worn out". He was really nice, a lovely old man.'

THE NEXT THING Marna got involved with was costume jewellery. 'It barely existed eighteen years ago. Nowadays you can buy jewellery for anything from £2.99 to a couple of hundred pounds and it looks a bomb. Again in a magazine, I saw where you could get these beautiful hand-painted ceramic beads. I made necklaces out of them, just for myself initially, but then people started asking me to make some for them.

'I started making them for the local country market in Ravensdale. My daughter Syro was captivated by the coloured beads and asked me to name them after her. So I did another label and wrote on it 'Syro Ceramics.'

MARNA THEN branched into wedding invitations. 'There was, and still is, a huge gap in the market. Wedding invitations are almost the same now as they were when I got married.

'A bride-to-be came along to me once and asked me to draw a scene from the area she came from for her wedding invitations. That's how it started. I would put the couple's names somewhere in the picture in tiny print, and hope that things wouldn't end up acrimoniously and they'd tear it up!

'I would also do a larger version and mount it for the couple to keep and I would make place cards with a slightly different view. Inside I would write "Remember us in your prayers".'

Marna has strong views about weddings. 'I actually think that weddings are barbaric. People go, they stuff their faces, and meet relatives they haven't met for a couple of years. They don't give the couple a flicker of a thought, other than the inconvenience of buying the present. Marriage is an appalling decision to make. It's a long life if it's not working out. I think all couples need a positive thought or a prayer.

'I got asked by so many girls to design wedding invitations. It just struck a chord. For four years after, when I had absolutely no time to do it, I was still asked.'

Marna would take the invitations to a monastery in Collon to be printed. 'I always had the kids in tow because they were still very young. I had four children at this stage. One of the monks at Collon said I should put a name at the back of the cards. We tried Trista, the third child, but that sounded awkward. So we picked on the eighteen-month-old, Dagan, and used the name Dagan prints.'

THE MAYONNAISE happened literally by accident. 'The country market that I was supplying was going to be visited by the committee of another country market and we decided to produce something a bit different to impress them. One of the girls said she'd had a beautiful garlic mayonnaise when she was in Spain the summer before, and we asked her if she would make it.

'She wouldn't because she had already tried and the mayonnaise had separated. She had looked in her liquidiser and seen probably £1.50 worth of ingredients gone down the tubes. She was wise but she was also shortsighted in being dominated by the idea that if you spend money you have to have some immediate return.

'There are a huge number of women like that and my husband would probably like it if I was more like that. But at the end of the day, it stops you having another go.'

Marna could remember her father making mayonnaise. 'He made it with a fork. If you've seen the speed a liquidiser has to go at to make mayonnaise, and even then sometimes it separates, I don't know how he did it, but he did and it was superb. I thought, if my dad could make it, it can't be that difficult.

'Late that Friday night, I made the garlic mayonnaise and it turned out a gem. I was going out of the door with it the next morning when Trista said, '"I've got nothing named after me". Nobody was thinking about business. I wrote Trista's Kitchen, on a label and drew another flower and she coloured it in.

'The first week the mayonnaise sold fine, the second week it sold fine, and the third week when I went to make it, at about midnight, it all separated. I stood looking at it, and I leaned back against the kitchen sink and I looked at it again to see had it improved, but sure it was worse and the next thing I poured the whole lot back out into a big jug and started from scratch. Before I knew it, instead of having eight jars I had 36.

'The girls at the market thought this was hilarious. I think women have an incredibly good sense of humour. I brought the extra into a delicatessen in Dundalk and into a fish and poultry shop. Both places began selling it regularly for me on a sale or return basis.'

MARNA THEN heard about the Industrial Development Authority through a friend who was doing a course on setting up in business. 'I rang up this guy at the IDA and if he had been dismissive I'd never have continued – there's a huge amount of luck involved. I went in to see him and I had boxes of stuff, I had figurines, I had necklaces. Some of these civil servants are real dry and they can be very pompous, but this guy wasn't. I had the mayonnaise, I had the wedding invitations. He looked at them all and he said, "Now what are we here to talk about?" and he took a fit of laughing.'

Dealing with the IDA was not without its difficulties. 'My biggest problem at that time was I didn't understand the terminologies. I regularly tell the IDA that they need to explain more clearly to new entrepreneurs exactly what it is they are getting in the way of a grant. If, like us, they are told they are being given a feasibility study for £15,000, then they go out of the door fully convinced that they are being covered for £15,000 and their bank has nothing to worry about.

'They nearly think they can walk on water, the adrenalin is hopping through the roof of their heads at this stage. What the IDA officials fail to recognise is that the person who has sat in front of them does not even understand the terms within which they're working. They don't realise that only certain receipts will be accepted and even these are put under a lot of scrutiny.

'We ended up spending £26,000 on developing the shelf life of the product. The IDA gave us something like £4,500. You can imagine the stress our relationship went through at that time. Michael, thank God, was as convinced as I was that we were going to get £15,000. Often the amount the IDA gives you only just covers the cost of presenting the goods to the IDA in the first place.'

Marna and Michael are still paying off the debt. 'We're paying it in bits and pieces. If we'd left the debt in the business, it would never have got off the ground.

MARNA RESEARCHED her market well. 'I went round the supermarkets and spoke to the buyers. I identified that there were no other flavoured mayonnaises. There was certainly no fresh mayonnaise in the chilled cabinet. It was the beginning of the wave of additive-free foods. I was interested in this because one of my children is hyperactive. I spoke to the back store men who check products in and check products out that haven't sold. The negative response that was coming back from the consumer was not to do with the price but with what they had to throw away.

'I took the advice of Anita Roddick of the Body Shop as far as packaging was concerned. She said, rather than conforming you should let your product stand out as being different from other products in the same line.

'We had major set-backs with research into the shelf life. We were working with one of the state bodies on this. We discovered not only that the IDA wouldn't fund "research and development" but also suspected that our research findings were being leaked to a rival company. In any event, we had difficulty in getting good confidential help in the development of the product.

'We would have spent about £18,000 at this stage. I felt very tired. You always feel tired when something seems insurmountable. It took me about two days to tell Michael. I'd put a lot on the line and he'd been quite tolerant about it, even though he'd been put under a lot of personal stress.

'I was doing terminal nursing at night at this time to help finances. I was also concerned to be around to help the kids with homework and music practice, so I was getting little sleep. I had a humorous, pleasant girl helping me out with the housework, and often I'd end up chatting to her rather than catching up on sleep.

'Late one night, when the kids were in bed, I told Michael. He was very analytical and detached. He decided things had gone far enough and we were to go to the bank and stop everything. The guy at AIB was, I think, amused by my personality and had backed me every step of the way, and we felt a loyalty to him. He used to come and sit in the freezing cold pilot plant where we were making the mayonnaise so that he could understand what we were at.

'The bank said we had to work out a system of paying back. I'd told the supermarkets that everything was on hold as we'd run out of money.'

'I was trying to work on the Trista project some evenings before I went to the night-nursing job. It was very lonely because I do enjoy the kids and my friends. There's never been a hint of begrudgery with my friends. They don't see me as anything to envy because they see how much work I have to put in.

Although things at this stage seemed very bleak, all was not lost. 'A cousin of Michael's who works for More Park in Fermoy, a research station closely aligned to University College, Cork, offered to help us out with the research at no charge. They salved our wounds and encouraged us to have a look at what we'd done without worrying about all the

money it had cost us. Within three or four months of working down there, we had the product on the shelf, with the
shelf life extended from four to six months.'

From then on, there was no looking back. 'We started
winning awards and getting articles written about us, and
we had a television programme made about us as well. As a
result, several companies approached UCC's dairy research
department and their budget was upped. That's the way
companies and educational departments should be oper-
ating.

'We won a Bank of Ireland IDA award in 1989 for being
the fastest developing business in the north-east. It increased our credibility with the banks and with the trade and it
gave us a lot of publicity. We've also won an AIB award.
One of the most valuable ones we won was *The Sunday
Tribune*/Glen Dimplex award. The whole thing was handled
live on the television by Pat Kenny.

'The corporate finance group, NCB, was one of the
judges and part of the prize was a year's free advice from
them. They said we should prepare a business plan, which I
did myself with the help of a step-by-step guide. For six
weeks I went into the Enterprise Centre, where Trista's was
based, at five o'clock in the morning to work on it.'

MARNA WAS KEEN to get the children involved so they
wouldn't just see the negative side of her having to work so
hard, and made sure they were invited to any award cer-
emonies. 'When Michael and I met with NCB to discuss the
business plan, I brought the children with me. That's one
thing that I never feel I should apologise for. I have brought
Syro, who would have been twelve or thirteen, into very
high profile financial meetings where there were discussions
about buy-outs and things like that and the men would be
so discommoded by this little blonde child sitting staring at
them and looking around the table.'

TRISTA'S TURNOVER IS now around £400,000. Over the last couple of years, the banks have been fighting over them and Marna has had a couple of offers of buy-outs.

'We were selling very well into London but our distributor went into liquidation so we're now concentrating on consolidating our business in Ireland first. We're now doing our own distribution across the whole of Ireland and that's working out very effectively for us. We supply Marks and Spencer in France, which is a good contract to have, especially as over this year and next year they are planning to open forty stores on the continent, covering Holland, Germany and Spain.

'We have two other products which we are looking at developing. It's hard to find the time and money for research and development, because it's extremely expensive. The product is moving very well at the moment.'

Wrapped up in the business as she is, with her husband as her business partner and the rest of the family also involved to a certain extent, Marna Fleming has little time off. She sometimes makes a point of separating work from family life. If she has a business matter of particular importance to discuss with Michael, she will arrange a meeting with him at a nearby hotel, so that the business element is paramount.

'Of all the things that have come a cropper, it's having time to spend with my friends,' she regrets. I hardly seem to have any personal time at all. I belong to a sports complex but never manage to get there. My friends have been so tolerant. I slot in with them once in a blue moon and they're there and they make me feel I've never been away.'

~ *Eight* ~

Mary Broughan

**Managing Director,
Woodchester Credit Lyonnais Bank
in Ireland
Company Secretary,
Woodchester Group**

MARY BROUGHAN was the first woman in Ireland to be appointed managing director of a licensed bank and the first woman executive director of a public company. In 1990, she was appointed Chairperson of the Pensions Board in Ireland and was the only woman in the Industrial Policy Review Group which published its report in May 1992.

She is more approachable than her status as managing director of Woodchester Bank might suggest. This in itself has probably been a key factor in her success. She is forthright without being confrontational. She has her own clear views, which don't block out the views of others. She listens well.

'I am not a feminist,' she warns, clearly bored with the 'woman in a man's world' routine, and dismisses any bearing being a woman might have on her everyday business dealings. 'In meetings I am merely one person dealing with other people.'

She appears confident and at ease with herself, but admits this was not always so. 'I went through all the stages of questioning myself many years back but the older you get, the more settled you get with yourself. You don't worry so much about what people think of you. What you think of people becomes much more important.'

WOODCHESTER BANK'S glossy new premises in Golden Lane, Dublin take up practically the whole street. They are on their third phase development there. 'We own almost the whole of Golden Lane at this stage,' said Mary. 'I think the pub on the corner is about the only bit that's left.'

The Woodchester group has expanded dramatically in a relatively short time, bringing its assets up to £1.5 billion. When Mary Broughan joined the firm in 1980, she was their twelfth member of staff and yearly profits were £50,000. Ten years later, it employed a staff of 800 and profits were £40 million.

'It happened gradually. When I first started working for Woodchester, it was very small, and all through the 1980s we grew both organically and by acquisition. We bought Hamilton Leasing in 1986, Bowmaker Bank in 1987, Trinity Bank in 1988 and Mercantile Credit in 1990.

'We are in the process of negotiating with UDT-First Southern Bank, which is owned by the TSB group in the UK. All these banks have been around a long time.

'I started with a company with twelve employees. In 1982, we went on the stock market, still a very small company. We raised £900,000, which at that time was a huge amount of money for us. In 1984, we made our first acquisition, a small finance company in Cork, which had about the same number of staff as we had. In 1986, we acquired Hamilton Leasing, our main competitor.

'It was small buying big. We had about twenty-five staff then and they had close to fifty. With the exception of seven or eight, they moved into this building and quickly integrated.

'The following April, we bought Bowmaker Bank which had 120 staff, so each time we doubled our number of people. We didn't have the specialist expertise of a personnel manager. We have lots of them now because we can afford them. When you're small you have to do a lot more for yourself.

'Most of our acquisitions were bigger than ourselves, particularly in the early days, so integration was important to retain the original Woodchester ethos. This was something we always had to strive very hard to achieve.'

Clearly a strong force in the moulding of this ethos, Mary Broughan is keen to stress the importance of teamwork. 'I would never see Woodchester Bank as a one-person bank. I have a very strong management team, some incorporated from other banks. My deputy managing director came from Bowmaker Bank and had been with them a long time.'

She denies having had to tread carefully around any egos during these mergers. 'Most of the people that I work with are very open. I always say what I think and I think people appreciate that. You know where you stand with some-body.'

Woodchester is 45% owned by Credit Lyonnais. 'We run the company, though we have regular dialogue with them.' The deal with Credit Lyonnais, concluded in January 1991, was hampered by the intervention of the British Secretary of State for Trade and Industry who referred the proposal to the Monopolies and Mergers Commission. The referral cost Woodchester and its shareholders approximately £5 million in lost interest. It also used up a lot of management time and delayed the group's European expansion plans.

Despite this setback, Mary Broughan has high hopes for the continued growth of Woodchester. 'We are a big bank. We'll have close to £1 billion in assets when we complete the UDT deal.' (This deal has since been concluded.)

Woodchester are looking to merge with a bank which has cheque book facilities, the only service they do not offer. 'We made a big effort last year to acquire the TSB. We have ten branches, and the UDT deal will bring this up to four-teen branches. For the business we run, this gives us good coverage nationwide without all the overheads of having a bank on every corner. We would like to have more branches but certainly not as many as AIB or Bank of Ireland.'

Woodchester are specialists in leasing. 'If you go to a garage to buy a car, you will more than likely be offered a finance package from Woodchester.' They have a base of around 250,000 customers and compete with the other banks in most areas except the cheque book. 'We don't have a current account; we have a deposit account, a loan ac-count, a lease account and various others. We are in the cor-porate end of the market and we have all the treasury ser-vices.

'We are currently working on raising the profile of the bank. We are probably the safest bank in Ireland for depos-its but people may not be aware of that. Credit Lyonnais are the fourth largest bank in Europe and they have guaranteed our liabilities.' (Since the interview, Woodchester Bank has changed its name to Woodchester Credit Lyonnais Bank.)

BORN INTO A farming family in Nenagh, Co. Tipperary, Mary is the second youngest of twelve children. Her parents are still hale and hearty at eighty-six. 'I grew up with eight brothers, seven of them older than me. Perhaps that's why I've never been intimidated by men,' she suggests. At seventeen, she left the Convent of Mercy to join the National Bank.

'I started at the bottom, as do most "career" bankers. I wasn't at all ambitious. I just went in to do a job. I was brought up to think if something's worth doing, it's worth doing well. In our house, if money was going to be spent on educating anybody it would have been spent on the boys rather than the girls. That was the norm at the time. Girls were expected to get married after a couple of years.'

The marriage ban, which prevented married women from working in the civil service, meant that Mary had to leave the National Bank in 1972. She accepted this with equanimity.

'The banks gave you a large gratuity when you got married and you needed the money. You looked at it as being money to furnish your house. You just left. Everybody did it and you didn't really think very much about it. The marriage ban was removed the year after. I knew it was going to be removed. I could have waited to get married but I didn't. I decided I would go out and get a job.'

Straight after her honeymoon, she went around the employment agencies and was offered two interviews – and two jobs. She chose the job with Hamilton Leasing, whose managing director was Craig McKinney, now Chairman of Woodchester.

IN 1977, Mary took three and a half years off work in order to start a family. She has two children, Jennifer and Paul, now aged fifteen and thirteen. 'I was asked to stay on. My response was that I knew I could do a job but I didn't know whether I could look after a baby and do a job as well.'

The week after her daughter started school, Mary went back to work. 'At the time I'm sure I felt very apprehensive but things worked out. I don't have any guilt pangs. I have a very good housekeeper who runs my home for me. She's been with me for ten years. Other than holidays, I don't think I've had to take a day off work. I've always had very good, reliable help.

'It's not one of the things you'll probably discuss with men but for a woman who's out working, or for a man who's part of a working husband and wife team, good back-up is essential. If it's not there, you won't be reliable. You won't be comfortable in the job you're doing if you're worrying that your children are all right.

'I can see how difficult it is for a lot of the young mothers I have working for me here. Most people now are working because they need to financially. Many have to leave children at crèches in the morning. It's a great strain. With one child it isn't too bad, but when there are more ... and then when they start to go to school it gets even more difficult.'

Mary's husband, John, is also in banking. A director of AIB capital market, he comes under the same sort of pressures as she does, which makes for a good understanding between them. They share responsibilities towards the children equally.

'AT WOODCHESTER, women have the same promotion prospects as men,' Mary Broughan insists. 'The best person gets the job. I probably have more women managers here than most organisations have. It doesn't come from a conscious effort to promote women but perhaps I don't have the prejudices that others might.

'We don't operate a positive discrimination policy towards employing women. I think most of the women who work for me accept that and would feel very bad about getting something just because they were female. They would feel it was patronising.'

She does admit, however, that employers tend to discriminate against women who have young children. 'Whether they admit it or not, they might consider that attendance and commitment levels will be affected. But I don't think you can assume that because somebody has a baby they won't be equally committed. Some people just make that extra effort.

'I have girls here in supervisory or management positions who have young children. They probably have to put a lot more effort in than their counterpart who has a wife at home looking after the children. But they do it.'

Despite the difficulties they face, Mary Broughan feels optimistic about prospects for working mothers. 'Things are changing. Women of my age had to give up work. Few would have gone back as quickly as I did. There were a lot of raised eyebrows at the time. People didn't exactly say I was neglecting my children, but the implication was there.

'That's why there aren't all that many women around who have automatically got fairly high up the ladder. Nowadays women often establish themselves in a career before they have children. If they have a responsible job they can sort something out with their partner beforehand. Some women will actually want to give up work and stay at home. I think that's great if that's what they want to do.

'People may say that's fine for me, I was lucky or things worked out a bit better for me than they did for a lot of other people. Obviously there is discrimination out there in some organisations, I have no doubt about that. I think that women have to work to show that they're just as good as everybody else to try and dispel it.'

FAMILY LIFE is a clear priority for Mary Broughan and she does her best to see that her long working hours do not impinge too heavily upon it. She always tries to keep her weekends free.

She seems relaxed, with no outward sign of executive

stress, though she admits that 'Maybe it's just a perception'. Her leisure activities balance out her heavy work load. 'I play tennis and I work out. I'm a member of Riverview and a tennis club. I read. I ski. We have a dog which has to be walked regularly. Family life is my main recreation.'

Mary admits that incorporating work and family life is easier if you have no money pressures. Otherwise, with little help from the state or employers, the working mother's lot is unlikely to improve dramatically. She is reticent, however, about who should intercede.

'I certainly would say that better facilities are required in Ireland. I don't know who should actually put them there. Should companies provide the facilities for working mothers? Maybe they should. We don't have facilities here at Woodchester. I don't know if it's the State's responsibility. I'm not big into saying the State should supply everything. I think people have a responsibility as well to look after themselves. Because the State is us. All of us.'

'I think the Government could certainly give a tax allowance for women who need to use crèches or employ somebody in the home in order to be able to go out to work. I am creating employment by employing somebody in the home but there is no allowance for that. And people are creating employment by using a crèche. I think the Government should certainly look at that.'

POLITICS HOLDS no attraction for Mary Broughan. 'It doesn't interest me at all. I'm too much of a private person. I do not know how anyone goes into politics.'

Policy making, however, is something in which she is involved on a national level. In December 1990, she became Chairperson of the Pensions Board, which published its first annual report in May 1992. 'We ensure that pension schemes are adequately funded and that when someone comes to retirement age, the pension they were promised will be there for them. There have been a couple of cases recently publicised where people were merrily paying into a fund all their lives and somebody else was taking the money out.'

Mary also gave up valuable free time to prepare the Industrial Policy Review report. 'I spent six months involved in the policy review group, making recommendations for industrial policy in the future. It was one of the most interesting projects that I've been involved in. It entailed a lot of work and heavy reading, not the sort of thing you'd generally choose to read on a Sunday afternoon.

'I was the only woman. I'm sure it was a conscious decision to have a woman on the board: "We have to have a woman so we'd better get one".' This thought amuses rather than angers her. She seems quietly confident that women will get there in the end.

MARY BROUGHAN, with her clear grasp of facts and figures and her accurate recall of information, makes being a successful businesswoman, even in an area as traditional as banking, seem surprisingly simple. Fair-minded and unassuming, she waves no banners and grinds no axe, and just by being in the position she is, probably does as much to further the case for women seeking advancement in the financial world as anybody else in Ireland today.

~ *Nine* ~

Mairead Sorenson

Joint Managing Director,
Butler's Irish Chocolate

AT THE AGE of twenty-two, Mairead Sorensen took over
her father's small chocolate company with her brother,
Colm, and has turned it into the biggest boxed chocolate
producer in Ireland. The company grew at a rate of 50%
each year for ten years. In 1990, they opened a shop in Grafton Street, Dublin and have expanded their factory in Pearse
Street, Dublin three times. Butler's Irish Chocolate now has
54 employees and supplies retail outlets all over Ireland, as
well as exporting to the UK, Italy and Germany. Their factory also makes the range of confectionery sold under the
Bewley's name.

Mairead trained as a nurse after leaving school. 'I don't
think there's a better training for business, because you
learn phenomenal discipline at a very young age. Between
the ages of seventeen and twenty, you are responsible for
other people, and you have younger trainees working under
you. A staff nurse has a tremendous amount of responsibility. She develops a memory for people and the ability to
do several different things at once.'

Mairead left for America and studied for the American
nursing exams, while working at nights and at weekends.
After a stint in Florida, where she worked in broadcasting –
reading the news on a radio station in Miami – and in public
relations, she returned to Ireland.

SHORTLY AFTER Mairead returned, her father died. He
had a small business, Chez Nous chocolates, which employed five people.

'We had to make a decision about what we were going to
do with the business. I have five brothers, all of whom were
at college. My mother was busy working, she was a doctor.
The first business commitment we had to meet was to provide a stand at the annual horse show at the Royal Dublin

Society. My father died in July and the horse show was the first week in August.

'Together with two of my brothers, who were on vacation from college, I prepared the stand. My brothers then went back to college and I stayed on running the business. My brother Colm was studying commerce so he helped me out with the financial end. He went on to become a chartered accountant and then came to work for the company full time.'

'Now I have two brothers here working with me, Colm, and Owen who joined in the last two years. I think working with family is wonderful. You get great loyalty and you're also used to dealing with them. You're used to having disagreements and getting over them.'

THE ELDEST of the family and the only daughter, Mairead has great respect for her mother. She didn't marry until she was into her thirties and had already had a chance to follow up her own interests. Then she had six children in eight years while continuing to work as a doctor.

'She had a full-time job and six kids and she was very happy. When I was going to school, I was the only person in my class with a working mother. We had all these debates about how you were going to be insecure if you were brought up by a working mother, you were going to be destroyed. The other little girls, who were about twelve or thirteen, were coming out with all these myths. I would say "I'm not insecure". I was very proud of my mother.

'She had help in the home and could also call on the extended family, grannies and aunts. It's a shame that this is becoming rarer nowadays. Mixed aged groups are healthy. I don't think older people should be isolated from younger people.'

BUSINESS WAS in Mairead's blood. 'I'd always been into trading even when I was at school. I think I'm naturally a trader. I would set up little businesses. When I was about seven, I cut up all the Christmas cards we'd received and took them into school. I sold them as holy pictures. Then I asked my mother if I could go out and buy a *Bunty* comic with the money. When she found out what I'd done, she made me give everybody back their money and let them keep the holy pictures as well. My father had a much more pragmatic attitude to it. He thought it was great.'

Mairead lived in America until she was three. Her parents were married there. 'My father worked as an accountant for RCA, the Radio Corporation of America. He bought the chocolate factory when he came home in 1959. We were brought up in a business household. The conversation at the table would often revolve around business generally.'

AT FIRST, Mairead had her doubts about working in a family enterprise. 'After teenage years, you want to bring out your own identity rather than going back into something your parents are involved in.' But the doubts were short-lived as she made her own mark on the company.

'We developed the business along certain lines. I probably made the packaging more feminine than it had been in the past – more ribbons and roses and that kind of thing. A lot of these things I would have seen abroad. Also I wanted to appeal to people of my own generation. Sometimes you look at your market and it's actually ageing way beyond your lifespan. Many of my customers were much older than I was and I needed new customers who were going to be around while I was around, so I could have a growing market.'

Mairead and her brother built up the business steadily from its base in Lad Lane. 'The most dramatic period of change was in 1986 when we moved premises to the IDA Enterprise Centre in Pearse Street. We changed our whole range of product. We moved from the English style of confectionery to Belgian-style chocolates. We changed the brand name, which was fifty-odd years old, from Chez Nous to Butler's Irish. We computerised all our accounts and everything we were doing. At the end of the year, we were exhausted.

'The Christmas in 1986 was the worst Christmas we ever had – and we should have been happiest. We'd been working for a year and a half to develop the new product range. We finally got it out in October of that year. We had moved into our new factory but we hadn't planned out how to use it yet. We had more space but we weren't actually using the space to make more chocolates. The product took off so well and we were on to such a winner that we couldn't make it fast enough.

'We were working seven days a week, on twenty-four-hour shifts to try and make enough stuff for Christmas, and we couldn't. We felt battered and exhausted and on top of that had to deal with complaints from customers who couldn't stock their shelves.

'Last year was the first year we didn't grow at the usual 50% rate. It was also the year we probably did the best. Growth is very expensive. It's very traumatic. It involves a lot of management time and energy.'

Butler's Irish now employs 54 people. 'The number of employees had increased year by year in keeping with our turnover. By 1986 we were falling out of the rafters at the Chez Nous premises in Lad Lane. We had 2,000 square feet there. We now have 12,500 square feet here. We took 4,000 initially then a further 6,000, then a further 2,500 square feet.'

THE BEWLEY'S CONNECTION began in 1989. When Campbell's took over Bewley's they brought with them a range of confectionery. Their manufacturing plant was not as efficient as Butler's but they had the edge on retail outlets. Colm Sorensen suggested a deal.

'It wasn't my idea. I hate parting with equity in anything. What I have, I hold. Colm went to Bewley's and he met Pat Campbell and talked to him. We did a deal. They had a chocolate company and we took that over with 30% of the equity in our company. We got the right to their name in all of their shops and also acquired what they already had in the way of manufacturing equipment.

'We made a separate range for them and we developed their existing products. There was cash involved as well. They paid us. It was a very good deal. We make the brands separately now and have different sets of customers for both brands. We have new ranges coming up shortly under the Bewley's name.'

THE ENTHUSIASM Mairead has for the business comes out when she describes how she feels at the launch of a new product. 'There's nothing like the excitement of putting a product out on the market. There's so much development and thought goes into something and then you put it on a shelf and walk away. Then you see the person, the consumer, coming along. When I'm standing at the airport sometimes and I see people looking at our stand, I have to hold myself back from going up and talking to them. "Why are you buying that? Who are you buying it for? Why have you picked that one in particular?" It's just fascinating. It's the biggest compliment anyone can pay you, to buy something that you've made and that you've designed.'

Not all the new products work but Mairead is not afraid to take the odd chance. 'For the size of our company, we have enormous scope to develop products. Maybe we're just not afraid to try something and see if it works. More things work than don't work. If it was the other way round, we'd be out of business.'

A self-confessed optimist, Mairead believes there is a positive side to getting things wrong. 'It makes sure you keep your humility. You know you don't always get it right. You have to be prepared to turn round and say, "I really screwed up. I got the market wrong".'

The Sorensens are about to break into a whole new market. 'We're bringing out a range of Bewley's chocolates now. We're doing a whole new development in packaging that will allow us into different types of outlets. We've always had a distribution problem because of the short shelf life of the product. You have to go into high turnover locations. This new range will allow us to compete with other boxed chocolates out of our usual niche.

'We're the biggest in a small niche market, but there's a whole market out there that we don't touch. So now we're going to be very small in a very big market – but you can keep going. You can develop accordingly.'

MAIREAD WAS more obsessed with the business at the beginning, than she is now. 'I had to be. But over the years I have learnt the value of delegation. I have excellent people and they have a lot of scope to do their own thing. They get more fulfilment that way and are more likely to want to stay.'

Small, market-oriented businesses fascinate Mairead. 'I think about business a lot, about other people's as well as my own. I'm not really interested in finance and banking, but in products and ways of getting things done and simplifying procedures.'

Money for its own sake holds no great interest for Mairead. While she enjoys the luxuries money can buy, she would hate ever to become dependent on them. She also finds that while it's easy to make money for a company, it's very hard actually to pay yourself. 'Most of my money would be in my business. I don't have very expensive habits and I don't intend to develop them.

'It's very hard to be rich in Ireland, legally. If you build up a company and then sell it, for example, you've got to give half of it back in capital gains tax. We all know the tax situation in this country is abysmal. I'm not very rich because I'm legal.

'The only people who seem to make any money are lawyers who work on tribunals. It seems very hard in Ireland to get things organised. Red tape seems to keep an awful lot of things down. But then again there is the mentality that, whatever system they come up with, everyone will try and abuse it. People are afraid to talk out against tax, and I'm almost afraid, because you feel you're going to bring the revenue commissioners down on your head.'

The present Government, Mairead considers, is ruining the enterprise culture. 'I've just come back from a meeting of the Small Firms Association. We were talking about the new finance bill. It seems that anybody who becomes a director is making themselves into a second-class citizen – the laws are so weird. People are saying that we have a problem with job creation but from the very top I think it's anti-enterprise.'

WOMEN, Mairead feels, make great business people, particularly in consumer goods. 'Women control most of the shopping. They know what they want. They know much better than men what things cost and what sells, and where there are gaps in the market, and they control most of the spending.

'Women have great attention to detail, and tenacity. They are also very creative. You need creativity in business because you have to have something that'll set you a little bit apart. You have to have a good idea. You need the tenacity to make sure the idea comes to fruition, and attention to detail to tie up the ends. Lateral thinking is another requirement.

'I think women make great salespeople. They are very honest. I have met women who have lied, but very few. I find that they really listen to what you want, too.

Women who work here can easily do two or three things at once. Men, I find, tend to be able only to concentrate on one thing at a time. You only have to think of a mother who can be on the telephone, feeding her kids, watching another child and having a dinner cooking all at the same time. Sometimes you ask a man to put in a nail and he wants you to stand behind him or get a hammer and help him. I always feel when you ask a man to do a job and he asks you to help him, he's taking all the good out of it.'

Men and women working together, she feels, make a great team. 'The combination of a male and female mind working on a project is very effective. They approach things in such different ways and interpret things differently. It is enriching when you have men and women really working at something together. You have different cards to play in negotiations and that can be a very powerful element.'

MAIREAD IS single, but likes the idea of having a family. If she were not running her own business, she feels, there's little she'd find as fulfilling as running a home. 'It's a management job and it's a creative job and you are your own boss. If I had a family, I would much prefer to be at home than be working in a dull job. My own home would be a business to me. I think the workplace is interesting for women and it gives them a lot of confidence, but I think that's only true if the job is a decent one. A lot of women have to work in awful jobs. I'd have much more fun at home with my family. I'd make it fun.'

~ *Ten* ~

Mirette Corboy

**Managing Director, Portland Estates
President, Construction Industry
Federation of Ireland**

WHEN Mirette Corboy was first elected president of the Construction Industry Federation of Ireland in 1981, she was the only woman in the world to hold such a post. Founded in 1935, the organisation includes more than 2,000 companies, covering everything from bricklayers to civil engineers, house-builders and furniture makers.

In 1992, Mirette was asked to take on the presidency again, and began her reign of office by engaging in a debate on the Maastricht Treaty, which was broadcast live around the country. She was on a panel with the presidents of the Federation of Irish Employers, the Chambers of Commerce and the Confederation of Irish Industry, who, together with the CIF, make up the four main business, industry and employer organisations in the country, representing firms employing 700,000 workers.

Mirette is a sympathetic and engaging woman, glad to be up there among the leaders of Irish industry and in a position to put forward the female view of things occasionally. Deeply conscious of the imbalance in a male-dominated business world, she is doing her best to even things up, working alongside organisations such as Network and the Council for the Status of Women, as well as being part of the Task Force on Unemployment.

THE ELDEST of four girls, Mirette was born and educated in Limerick. After school, she attended the Sorbonne in Paris, where she studied French language, history and art. She worked as a courier and interpreter for a while, then married a Limerick man, Seán Hanley.

'I married an engineer. He was in charge of developments for the local authorities, housing developments. He was most anxious to break out on his own and start up a property business. A few months after our marriage, we decided to do that,' said Mirette. While her educational background was purely cultural, Mirette was no stranger to financial matters, for her father was a bank manager. She and her husband worked well together and the business grew.

'In the early days when the children were small, I worked part-time in the business. I took care of PR and did all the interior décor for the show houses. But I was also involved in the acquisition of land, which is an intrinsic part of running a housing company. In those days, we were developing and expanding the firm.'

By the mid-1970s, Portland Estates was one of the largest house-builders in the mid-West area. Having started with an office behind their house, and a work force of five, Mirette and Seán Hanley ended up employing 120 direct operatives as well as some contractors.

'Subcontracting was not as important a part of the industry as it is today. We employed a few, such as electricians, but the majority of our staff was employed on a full-time, permanent basis. No company would dream of doing that today because of the cyclical nature of our business,' explained Mirette. 'Contracts don't last. Housing estates begin and end. But in those days, in family firms particularly, you took on people and you got to know them and you got to know their wives and their families and you carried them through good times and bad times, which the media and the government departments didn't always remember. There were good days but there were certainly very low ones when you carried a huge direct staff.'

IN 1973, Mirette's husband died very suddenly. The company had been going twelve years and she had three children. 'It was an appalling shock. I don't think I ever really hesitated. I don't think I had a choice but to go on. Because by the nature of a construction company and a house-building company you are committed to land acquisition, you have a land bank, you're already into fees with architects and engineering companies who'd be surveying the lands. You'd also be dealing with the local authority over planning permission and so on.'

Mirette met the men on site after Seán's burial and told them that she would be carrying on. From then on, she became totally involved in the running of the company. At this stage, her two sons were eight and twelve, and her daughter was ten. She concentrated on finalising several major deals that had actually been on the cards, and then set about building up her professional qualifications in the construction field.

'I took a lot of courses with the Irish Management Institute and with the business development unit of the CIF with regard to on-site management and financial structures, things which I thought I should brush up on, even though I had a day-to-day practical knowledge of them.

'I would come up to Dublin maybe three days a month for a period of a year and study and do papers on various subjects. Eventually I was made a fellow of the Institute of Quantity Surveyors.'

Mirette had little free time. 'I was fortunate in those days because I had a very devoted housekeeper. My eldest boy and my daughter were at boarding school. I always had my weekends with the children and we always had our holiday periods together.

She realises that other women are not always so fortunate. 'I'm acutely aware of how badly a good network of child-care is needed for the changed position of women today. So many of them now go out to work that the shortfall in help available is appalling. That's a matter we're dealing with on the Task Force on Unemployment. I represent the CIF on the task force and child-care is one of the matters on the agenda. It has to be brought off the black economy, and child minders have to be paid a just wage. And I think that will come.'

THE TASK FORCE on Unemployment was set up by the then Taoiseach, Charles Haughey, for a group of the heads of industries to find ways and means of creating employment. 'It's been going now for a full year and meets nearly every week. Certainly we haven't come up with any extraordinary miracles but we have placed thousands in jobs. So we have helped to keep the number of people on the live register down. Hopefully we will continue. There are twelve pilot areas throughout the country where we are trying to bring people off the long-term register. There are a lot of things going on that won't show immediate results but it's nice to know this work is continuing on a weekly basis.'

MIRETTE HAS changed the structure of her own company, allowing her to broaden her focus. 'My children weren't interested in the construction industry. Construction has changed its very nature and is now all subcontracting. I had to take a very positive decision in the early 1980s that I would unload the workforce and make men redundant. A lot of them were at an age where they didn't mind. They'd been with us a long time. We had records of men who had twenty years' employment with us. I was able to lay them off gradually. It is a very costly thing to do.

Today I feel I have much more control of my life. Before, a lot of the work was created simply because there were so many people involved in the company. I have shifted direction slightly now, partly as a result of the experience I gained through certain legal cases. I went through some unusual cases in the building arena. One of the arbitrations that was held in connection with land that I had is now cited in Law. Now, that wasn't very exciting for me but it gave me a lot of experience in the problems that could arise in several planning areas. I saw an opportunity to concentrate on the development of the land that I had left. I also saw that there was a lot of demand for property consultants. Today I act as a property developer and a property consultant.'

Mirette now runs Portland Estates with her second husband, Anthony Corboy, whom she married six years after Seán's death. 'I have three stepchildren but we don't call them stepchildren. That was a decision we all made. I married a man from Limerick. Our parents know each other. He had known my husband and I had known his wife, who also died tragically. He gives me great backing. He's a businessman himself. He was the founder of Spar in Ireland and had also been involved in property. He has come totally over to my area of work now.'

In what could only be seen as a devastatingly cruel blow of fate, Mirette Corboy lost her second husband in July 1992, just a few weeks after this interview took place, when he died suddenly from a blood clot to the heart.

MIRETTE HAS rarely felt that men have tried to intimidate her for being a woman in an area of work which is more predominantly male than most. When she first took over the company, however, there were some difficulties. 'In the days when industrial relations were not great, one or two people did try to take me on in that area to see how far they could push me. They did try to push me and there were nasty things done. But I took them on. I went through the procedures, I went through the tribunals and I generally won. In the history of the company, we have never had a full-scale strike. We have a very good record.'

She hopes that her working life has not radically altered her personality. 'I remember a very dear friend saying to me when I first decided to take over the company: "I'll ask you one thing, do it if you feel it won't change you as an individual totally". I was always conscious of that advice and I tried not to let it happen. I've always tried to keep my private life and the way I think a little separate from work. Your attitudes have to change but I hope that I have never brought anything home.'

MIRETTE NEVER really considered not working outside the home. 'I never had the opportunity to stay at home. But I don't think I'd have been satisfied. Even at home, I love doing things with the house. I love gardening. I love music. I've always been involved in a charity of some kind, particularly those that relate to children. I chair the Limerick Youth Service Board for Sister Joan Bowles. She's a wonderful person and does an enormous amount of work for the underprivileged and abused of the city of Limerick. She's a shining star and I'm proud to chair that board for her.'

Mirette is also actively involved with Limerick University. 'I was on the first governing body. I was always a great believer in keeping the university alive at night. I'd said to the governing body over the years that with all the beautiful grounds and trees, we should see some way of bringing the students on to the campus. One day, he rang me and asked me to do this. We set up a small company, which in fact became quite big, and he asked me to run it.'

The company, called the Plassey Campus Centre Ltd, devised a means of putting up student residencies which was copied by Dublin, Cork and Galway. 'The idea originated with us and we're very proud of it. We've now just completed 420 houses. I love to be involved in the university and what's happening there. It really is a place of excellence and achievement and accomplishment. It's lovely to be a small part of that.'

As president of CIF, Mirette will be kept busy travelling around the country. 'We have fourteen branches throughout Ireland. Sometimes they feel that everything is concentrated round the Dublin area. This morning in the broadcast on the Maastricht Treaty, I addressed Mayo, Sligo, Laois, Offaly, the mid-West, Cork and Waterford about what was going on in their own areas. I stressed the importance of the cohesion fund in helping us build our infrastructure and open up the West to Europe. These are the regions I will be travelling around and so it was nice to have an opportunity to speak on radio to them.'

DESPITE RUNNING her company and all her other involvements, Mirette comes across as a relaxed and happy person. 'I find it easy to wind down. I don't switch off suddenly but I wind down gradually. We have a home in Kilkea which is just an hour's run from Limerick. I find the walks and the sea air and the ocean have a calming effect.'

Her philosophy on work is simple. 'I always try to do a job to the best of my ability. If you win, you win, and if you lose, you lose. If you lose, you get up and you start again. Success comes if you're dedicated enough and if you're persevering enough – and if you make things happen. You have to make things happen. You can't sit back and wait for them to happen without nudging them in the right direction.

'In the construction industry, it's peaks and valleys, ups and downs. It is not the easiest of industries to be in. But on the other hand, it's rewarding and you can get a sense of fulfilment out of it. It's not a routine, boring business because you deal with so many people: the people you employ, the local authority, the CIF, the law, the bank. You need at least some basic knowledge of every area. You have to know about land, about building and building regulations. It's complex but it's certainly not boring.'

WHILE INFLUENTIAL in several areas of policy making, Mirette has never been tempted by politics. 'I have been asked to go into politics but I said no. I had no ambitions in that direction. I think I'd prefer to be able to say what I wanted to say, and not what I had to say.'

One area in which she is taking active interest is education. 'Now there are programmes to take care that girls in the latter part of secondary education can do honours maths, technical drawing and the subjects they would need to get into the construction industry. There are two EC-backed programmes drawn up in conjunction with the Department of Education to that effect, and they are in place now. It's important to see that they are carried through and that girls are made aware of them. I will certainly be monitoring the outcome in terms of third-level subject take-up. They have the potential and they have the ability to go into different areas. They are thrown back into a pattern from which they have to emerge to take a full part in life and in the growth of this economy. The contribution from women is badly needed to give the proper balance.'

Mirette sees a great future for women in the construction industry. 'There's a lot of good work being done by women. I recently addressed the Dublin branch of Network in Jury's Hotel, and I was amazed at the interest in an area which is generally not seen as being suitable for women. We had a terrific turnout. The questions and answers had to be stopped, and we still stayed on late in the evening and we've had follow-up ideas.

'There is interest and there are possibilities because the construction industry has changed and there are a lot of areas that women would be interested in. I'd like to encourage women to come into the construction arena. It is very challenging and satisfying. In our area, you generally see the end product and you have an end result.

'A lot of Irish firms are small firms and there's always a woman somewhere there doing the books, or doing the pay, or backing up the operations. I know a lot of businesses where the woman is the mainstay even though she might not be to the forefront. She's there in the background all the time seeing that things get done. Women are persistent and dedicated and better communicators than men. I'd like to see more of them come to the fore.'

~ *Eleven* ~

Eileen Gleeson

Managing Director, Financial and Corporate Communications

EILEEN GLEESON considers that heading her own Public Relations company at the age of thirty-one is no big deal. Yet she is among only a handful of women who have made it to the top in PR, even though it is a fairly new field which has attracted more than its share of women. The PR Consultants' Association, a forum for the heads of PR companies, chaired by Eileen in 1990, includes just 8 women to 22 men.

'I'm not a trailblazer,' Eileen said. 'There were lots of women in PR before me. There were also women who had their own companies and women who were managing directors, so it didn't seem like anything different. There have always been women in PR and a lot of people say that women are better at it. But at the same time, if you look at the list of the PR companies in Ireland, the majority are still owned and run by men.

'This is definitely the last generation where that will be the case,' Eileen continued. 'With the number of women coming through the ranks they will probably soon outnumber the men at the top. It's a pity in a way. While I don't like to see 22 men to 8 women, neither would I like to see 22 women to 8 men. It's nicer in any industry to have a good balance.'

The first PR companies were mostly set up by men who had been journalists, Eileen explained. They then employed women as secretaries. The organising skills of these women quickly became apparent and they were soon closely involved in running the firms.

IT WAS THE legendary long lunch which first enticed Eileen into PR. Her father owns Gleeson's pub in Booterstown Avenue, Blackrock, Co. Dublin. 'Lunchtimes were always very busy and there'd be a big contingent of media people. It was the days when long lunches were part of the job.'

Eileen worked in her father's pub while repeating her Leaving Certificate. She wanted to get enough points to do Law, her first career choice. 'I used to watch all these people coming in for their long lunches and thought what a wonderful life they had. They'd be there for about three hours and their offices would phone them with any messages. Then they'd go back and sign a few letters before going off to their receptions in the evening. I remember asking one of the older staff at the pub what they actually did. "They're in PR," he replied. I said, "That's what I'd like to do".'

Things didn't quite work out as Eileen had hoped. 'By the time I started working in PR the long lunch had gone. Now you rarely take lunch and only go out if you have to.'

Eileen took a course in PR at the College of Commerce in Rathmines, Dublin, having spent some time travelling around Europe on her own. At one stage she worked in a hotel which was full of limbless German War veterans taking their annual holiday. 'I ended up being half a nurse and half a waitress.'

Having saved some money from this job, she continued her travels. 'Never once did it worry me that I was on my own. Neither did I think, "This is really good of me", or "I'm being very independent". Maybe I just don't think about things as I'm going through them.'

Meanwhile her mother had been keeping an eye out for PR courses on offer, which were few and far between in 1979. 'When I got in touch with my mother she said I'd better come back as interviews for a course in PR were to be held the following week at the College of Commerce in Rathmines. I came back without a clue what PR was, apart from the long lunch. I had a week to find out and even when I got on to the course I only had a vague idea of what it was about.'

Towards the end of the year's course, Eileen was offered a part-time job in PRI, Public Relations of Ireland, who gave her a full-time job when she qualified. 'I went straight in. At the time there were jobs around.'

At about the same time, Eileen, who is a gifted singer and

harpist, was offered a job playing in a group in Bermuda. 'My boss at PRI would joke that I joined his company rather than going off to the Bahamas to play music. There was some truth in this. There was a group going over to the Bahamas to play in a hotel and they needed an Irish harpist. But it would only have been for six weeks and very poorly paid, so it wasn't really an alternative. I may have chosen Bermuda if the job offer had been more attractive.'

Eileen started in the company as a trainee account executive. She appreciated not having to go in as a secretary and work up. 'It's a difficult leap to leave behind being a secretary. It would probably have been more difficult then than now. I don't think there's the same demarcation now between secretaries and trainee account executives. Most come from the same educational backgrounds and have the same abilities. It's down to who has the most "cop on" and who is the most streetwise at the end of the day. In many cases this will be the person who has come from a secretarial school rather than the person who's come from doing a degree in a protected environment.

'When I started work, my plan was very simple. I was a trainee account executive and I wanted to be an account executive. When I got to be an account executive a year later, I said, "Now I want to be an account director". It was just a small thing. It wasn't as if I wanted to take over the world. When I achieved that, I said, "Now I want to be a director of the company". I just made small moves going from one stage to the next. There was no big leap. I became a director in 1986.

'It was a small company with a close-knit team. The promotions didn't make any difference to the work I was doing and very little difference to the pay. It was only really the title that changed. But with a better title you can achieve a little bit more and demand a little bit more.'

Most of Eileen's first accounts were consumer products. 'I worked on Wrangler jeans, and though I loved the idea of working in fashion, I hated it in practice. I found it quite disconcerting having to go around with glamorous models!'

Another early assignment was to organise the 21st birthday party for the staff of Superquinn supermarkets. 'The brief that Fergal Quinn gave us was that he wanted his staff and their families to do things which they had never done and would never hope to do in any one day, in a place which they would never normally visit. Around 2,000 people were to be invited and we worked on the idea for six months.

'We hired Desmond Guinness' estate in Leixlip and built a tented village there. This was quite a new idea at the time. We arranged for different types of entertainment to be going on simultaneously and employed a huge staff of young people to help out, dressed up in strange costumes. It was great experience in organisation and was great fun.'

Eileen's enthusiasm for organising events like this has waned during her time in PR. 'That is a line of work I don't do now at all. I no longer enjoy doing that sort of work personally. I leave it up to other people.'

Eileen now much prefers consultancy work. 'Every company, no matter what size it is, has a range of audiences who have an influence on its business. These generally include their employees, their customers, their suppliers, the general public, the local community, the unions, the government. The company needs to communicate in one way or another with each of these audiences. People need to feel informed enough to make a decision about that company. Usually the more informed they are, the better their perception of that company will be.

'Some companies are well tuned into PR and may just want you to tackle a specific problem area. Other companies have never really considered PR before, apart from organising functions, perhaps, and need to talk through the whole concept of corporate communications. In fact I called my own company Financial and Corporate Communications.'

Eileen loves planning and implementing PR strategies. 'We ask the company what they would like each of their audiences to think of them and then we work out how to achieve this. We work out ways of being more informative and more open, whether it's through print material, open days, sponsorship, corporate entertainment, publicity, advertising, direct mail, or however. You work out a plan. I love doing that. It's just A, B and C. I find it so simple.'

On the financial PR side, Eileen has worked for companies such as Ryan Hotels, helping them announce preliminary and interim results, organising annual general meetings and annual reports to shareholders and working with them on investor relations.

Another side of financial PR is dealing with takeovers or mergers, an arena which Eileen enters with much enthusiasm. 'It's great fun because you become totally immersed in a project for a specified period of time. You have to eat, drink and sleep it. I did a few of them when I was working for Public Relations of Ireland. We worked for Irish Distillers when there was a hostile takeover plan. We were defending Irish Distillers. We moved into their offices and didn't leave for six months. We had our own office and our own telecommunications system there.'

Eileen also worked for Abbey, a property company in England, when they were trying to avoid being taken over. The company is owned by Charles Gallagher, part of the well-known Irish Gallagher family. 'He's a really strong person and from the first day he said, "This is a battle. Who's on our team?" We'd meet in the morning and in the evening to discuss tactics and analyse what the other side had done. It's almost like being involved in a political campaign. It's a game of strategy.'

Eileen set up her own company partly to be able to specialise in the type of business which interested her most, but mainly because there was no next 'little step' she could take at PRI.

'I was a director of a company where there were two other directors, both of whom were shareholders and partners. There was no way that I was going to be able to take over and run that company. It was a choice between going to work for somebody else or setting up on my own. At that stage, I didn't think I'd be able to go and work for anybody

else because I was so used to working with my colleagues
and we got on so well together. PR is a strongly competitive
world. You become very protective of the company you are
in. I'd have felt very awkward going off to join the next biggest PR company.'

For a while, Eileen swung between counting her bless-
ings where she was and feeling the urge to start up on her
own. 'I would go through a period of thinking, "Why do I
want to go through the heartache of starting up on my
own?" Then a couple of months later, I'd say, "Why don't I
go and do it myself if I'm working this hard for other people?"'

This second option crystallised during a rainy holiday in
Tenerife. At the end of the six months' period based at Irish
Distillers, Eileen decided to take a break away with her husband, Gerry. 'It was November. We went to the travel agent
and just asked for anything going out in the next three days.
We ended up in Tenerife, and we had dreadful weather.
This didn't bother me for the first week because I was just
sleeping, I was so tired. Then I decided to use the next two
weeks really to make up my mind about whether I wanted
to set up my own company or not.

'I wrote the business plan and worked out a list of questions. Gerry didn't want the project to be totally consuming
me. So we had an arrangement that there would be ten minutes' discussion about it every day and if I had any questions or opinions to ask of him, I'd do so in those ten minutes, and that was it. No other discussion. No pondering
and wondering. By the time I came back I had decided that I
would go for it.'

Armed with her business plan, Eileen focused on planning her new company. 'My brother is an accountant and
my brother-in-law is a tax consultant, so I had good advice. I
gave in my notice after Christmas. Then I approached Mary
McCarthy who was an associate director of the company.
She and I had worked closely together on accounts. She had
come from the secretarial end and had become a PA. I knew
that she could work as a PR person and at the same time

was able to work on the administrative side, she would keep the company together. She would know about finding desks and how much stationery we would need and things like that.

'Mary thought about it for a week and then agreed to join me. There was initially some friction with the partners. It was completely understandable from their point of view. They were losing two people. We left quite quickly after that and didn't work out our notice. We're now very good friends with both of them, but it was awkward at the time. I was taking some clients with me. But only those with whom I had worked exclusively. I didn't poach any of their clients.

'We started with four companies and built up from there. We hadn't had time to sort out an office or stationery but as we already had clients we had to get going immediately. A friend of a friend offered us a spare office in his premises in Fitzwilliam Square. He didn't want any rent and he gave us phones for free. We spent six weeks there and then found offices in Fitzwilliam Street, where we stayed for three years. Last month we moved to our own building on Clanwilliam Terrace where we will have room to grow.

'The company was set up in February 1989 – on Saint Valentine's Day. On the first morning, we borrowed two desks from a business equipment dealer. I rang him and said, "We're going to start a company and we're going to be buying loads of furniture from you in the future, but for the moment could we just borrow two desks?" So he lent us two desks, two chairs, a photocopier and a fax machine. For the first month we didn't have to lay out anything for equipment.'

Eileen was also lucky with her clients, many of whom offered to pay her in advance. She then approached the bank for a loan. 'I had geared myself up and worked out a big presentation. I was in with the bank manager for about an hour and at the end of the meeting all he asked was how I felt about discrimination against women in the workplace. I said, "What's that got to do with me setting up my own business?" He said, "Well, if you feel strongly about things like that, don't you think it will affect your work?"

'I couldn't make any sense of what he was saying. Maybe he was trying to get to some very important point, but there was I talking for an hour about equity and shareholding and overdrafts and accounts – things my brother had rehearsed me in for nights – and all he was interested in was discrimination against women.'

As it turned out, money was not a problem. 'I had followed my brother's advice in asking for an overdraft facility rather than a loan and in fact we never even had to use the overdraft facility, except once when we went overdrawn by 37p by mistake.

'There was a lot of goodwill from clients and suppliers. We would laugh and joke about having to look for jobs if it didn't work out. We didn't really take it terribly seriously. We took the business seriously, but we didn't panic on the first day about where we'd be in three years' time.

'Most men would find it difficult to have this attitude, and with reason. I knew that if the business didn't work I would just get another job. I knew that Gerry was always going to be in employment – he's in the Irish army. We don't have children. For a man with a wife at home and a family to support, it would have been harder. At the same time, I think that no matter how seriously you have to take business, you can still retain some element of fun and not let it panic you completely.

'I didn't think that if the business failed in the first year my pride would be hurt. I would have been able to say to myself, "Well, I gave it a shot". It was only after the first year in business that failure would really have meant something. When people start forming opinions about the existence of your company then it becomes harder to treat it as something that's just fun. You have to think more seriously about where it is and how it's developing.'

After less than a year running her own company, Eileen was appointed director of the press centre at Dublin Castle, overseeing publicity and helping to organise events for Ireland's EC presidency year.

'When I became chairman of the Public Relations Consultants' Association, in our second year of business, I felt that nothing could go wrong with my company then because it would be an awful reflection on PR.'

Financial and Corporate Communications now employs six people. 'The most I would like to grow would be by another two or three people, so that it would be big enough while remaining manageable. PR companies traditionally don't become massive.

Eileen compares running her own business to 'going up one side of the ladder and coming down the other. I feel there are a couple of extra steps to go and then I'd like to have the chance to become less involved with the company, at least with the day-to-day running of it.'

EILEEN'S CORPORATE involvements outside her own company include being on the boards of the National Lottery and the National Concert Hall. Political involvement holds no attraction for her.

'I've never wanted to go into politics. I think because I know so much about what they do. I've worked with politicians a lot. I cannot understand how anyone would want such a hard job. People complain about politicians being paid so much and doing so little, yet most of them work really hard, with very little thanks.'

The lack of a clear career path in politics also puts Eileen off. 'There are too many outside influences. If I said I want to be a county councillor, then a senator, then a TD and then a minister of state, I wouldn't be able to do that because I wouldn't be in control. If you're a TD, no matter how well you do things, if somebody doesn't like you or if somebody doesn't like your party or one thing that you get involved in, then you've blown it.'

HER FAMILY BACKGROUND, Eileen feels, has played a major part in her success as a businesswoman. 'My parents both worked. My mother looked after the food side of the pub. They had eight children and I'm in the middle of them. We'd each receive great encouragement for what we were good at, it didn't have to be something academic. My sister would bake a nice cake and there'd be great celebration. If I got a prize at the Feis for singing and playing the harp, there'd be great celebration for that. It was every one to their own.

'Most of us are now involved in people-related business-es. Because we lived beside a pub there were always people around. It was like Heuston station. My father thought it was important for our development to be able to interact and get on well with people. He would consider it as im-portant to be able to hold a good conversation as to get an A in maths.'

EILEEN SEES women making their mark more and more in the business world. 'It's going to happen. It's not going to happen because a president or a Taoiseach or the chairman of an industry body stands up and says that next year we're going to employ 60% women. It's not going to happen by quotas. If quotas come in, fine, that will be a good thing. But it's not going to happen because of those. It's going to hap-pen anyway and it's going to happen as much because of women themselves as it is because of men.

There are always going to be men who are discrimi-natory. I know the look. Sometimes I'll walk into a room and they look at me as if to say, "What is this young girl doing coming in here to talk to me about my business?" It's just a look but you can see it quite clearly in their faces. You just write off that sort of person because they're not going to change and you're not going to change them. What is the point of trying? They're the people who are going to be left behind at the end of the day. There are going to be more of us than there are of them.

'There are definitely some businesses where it's very hard for women. I know that. But it's up to women them-selves and we're going to get there. It's going to happen.'

~ *Twelve* ~

Marie Cooney

Director,
Tipperary Natural Mineral Water

AFTER NINE YEARS as a housewife and mother, Marie Cooney came out into the business world and has established her product, Tipperary Natural Mineral Water, across Ireland and in 13 other countries, including the United States, Russia and Australia. Six years after the launch of the product, Tipperary is now a high profile brand name. It is served on all Aer Lingus flights as well as in hotels, restaurants and pubs. Bottled water coolers dispense Tipperary Water in offices and workplaces throughout Ireland.

In 1991, Marie branched out and launched Tipperary Facial Mist in conjunction with Bronwyn Conroy cosmetics. The spray is now included alongside Gucci products in airline travel packs, as well as appearing widely on retail cosmetic shelves.

Marie gets great satisfaction from capturing new markets. 'I've just returned from Amsterdam where I acquired an agent who has established us in all the top class restaurants in the city. He has also got the water on to Lufthansa airlines going out of Holland and Belgium,' she says, delighted with her latest coup. 'When the planes refuel, the water goes on board and is carried on to Germany, Cyprus and Malta.'

At forty, Marie feels, 'Life has just taken off. It's been a whole new lease of life for me. 'It's been absolutely fascinating. I would not do it unless I enjoyed it. It has introduced me into so many exciting fields. My brain has started to work properly again.'

MARIE IS FROM a farming background, one of ten children. Her father owned a farm in Co. Meath and her mother had her own 350-acre farm in Lusk, Co. Dublin. Her mother was taken out of boarding school to run the farm herself after the death of Marie's grandparents.

When Marie and her husband, Patrick, first married, they moved to Tipperary and set up a wholesale bottling business. At first they distributed bottled drinks for other manufacturers, then started manufacturing their own soft drinks.

Marie had been working in a publishing house in France when Patrick proposed. Having left boarding school, which she attended from the age of nine, she wanted to follow a career where she could incorporate her love of languages and travel. While in France, she was offered another job in Greece. Patrick's proposal cut short her travels, bringing her back home to Ireland and to Borrisoleigh, Co. Tipperary.

'I had a complete change of direction. To this day I love travelling. I would travel anywhere at the drop of a hat, though it's very difficult when you have lots of children.' Marie now has five children, two daughters, aged fifteen and thirteen, and three sons, aged eleven, seven and three. 'I came back to live in a little village. We were building a house in Borrisoleigh and lived first of all in Templederry, a tiny village right up in the mountains. Just a door and two windows. It was a massive change from my life in France.

'I was always busy doing things. I was always into something: French polishing, flower arranging, Cordon Bleu cookery courses. I helped Pat out a little with the business. We distributed bottled beer to hotels, pubs and restaurants from our depot in Borrisoleigh. Then we decided we would go into the manufacture of soft drinks. There were grants available for soft drinks at the time.'

The Cooneys sank a well in 1979. They needed their own source, as the mains supply in the village would not have met the requirements of soft drink production. 'We had to bring in a big drilling unit,' Marie explained. 'It cost an absolute fortune. We got a diviner in, the Twin Young, he was called. He went round with his sally stick and he found the well under a mobile unit which we had been using for office work. We went down 300 feet and there was nothing. The Twin Young assured us there was water there. He convinced Pat to go down another 50 feet, and just after the 300 foot mark, we struck water.'

Marie had four children in fairly quick succession and was not involved with the business to any great extent at first. It was only when they decided to enter the bottled water market that her business acumen really came to the fore. She remembers how they decided upon the name Tipperary.

'We were on holiday in Egypt, on an incentive trip organised by Cantrell and Cochrane, one of the larger soft drink producers. I was pregnant with my fourth baby at the time. We were travelling down the Nile and the group included five or six different nationalities. The captain asked us to do a party piece for the last night. There were six Irish couples and we were having a wild time. We dressed up in long green jellabas and sang, "It's a long way to Tipperary". All the different nationalities knew the song and joined in with the chorus. Pat said, "That's the name we should use for our water".'

The name certainly struck the right note. 'Now, no matter where I exhibit, in Germany, France, Holland, I'll get people coming up to the stand singing, "It's a long way to Tipperary". The name was right. People remembered it.'

After they returned from Egypt, Pat asked Marie to help him market the water. 'I went up to Scotland to exhibit at a food fair. I had a five-month-old baby at this stage. I spent a week in Scotland and had a wonderful time. I enjoyed being involved in a new product. Bottled water was just beginning to take off and become big business. I met a lovely girl up there who worked for a company called Strathmore Water, which was also just starting up in business. A couple of weeks ago, Strathmore sold out for £11 million.

'I was inspired by her business card which featured a Scottish castle, and came home and designed our own label depicting the Rock of Cashel and the Devil's Bit.'

Marie's next task was to establish Tipperary Water with the restaurant trade. 'I started two days a week doing the rounds of the restaurants. I would go out, all dolled up, with my little bottle of water and my brief case and my price list. I would literally walk from one end of the street to the other, going into all the restaurants. Sometimes it would be marvellous and the people would be very nice, and other days you'd get rejections. Six years ago water did not have such a big market as it has now.

'I didn't pluck up the courage to try the hotels for a while. Having been out of business for so long and out of the habit of work, it took me a while to build up my confidence.'

Now Marie takes care of the mineral water while Patrick concentrates on the rest of the business. They bounce ideas off each other and attend advertising meetings together. A television commercial has recently been produced for the mineral water.

In 1992 the water won the British Bottlers' Institute Gold Medal in the still mineral water class. The competition attracted 210 entries from UK and foreign producers and was judged by blind tastings.

It was Marie's idea to branch out into the facial mist, which she has now established on the market, having overcome initial difficulties with the canning procedure. In 1992 she signed a deal with a trading house to have the mist put into travellers' packs for first class air passengers.

THREE YEARS after becoming fully involved with the business, Marie became pregnant with her fifth baby. 'I was quite ill at the time and very tired, but I knew that I wanted to continue with the work. I didn't want to stop. I enjoy the excitement of it so much.'

The excitement is counterbalanced by a lot of hard work. Marie works from her home in Donabate. 'Pat has often asked me to come into the office,' she said. 'But I feel that would be giving up. Working from home I'm not distracted. I can concentrate on "my" product. If I was in the office, I'd probably end up getting involved in other aspects of the business.'

The company as a whole has flourished since the sinking

of the well in 1979, with premises in Ballyfermot, Dublin, as
well as the plant in Tipperary. It now employs 300 people
and is part of the Gleeson Group of companies, the third
largest soft drinks producer in Ireland after Coca Cola and
Cantrell and Cochrane, a subsidiary of Guinness.

'I'M VERY DILIGENT in what I do,' said Marie. 'I start at
quarter past nine, when my housekeeper comes in, and fin-
ish at quarter past five. Last week I did all the organising for
a race we were sponsoring at Drogheda's Bellewstown
Races. That meant arranging everything from tickets, tro-
phies and local radio interviews to catering and flowers.

'I have to stop work when the housekeeper leaves and
then I take over the care of the younger children. Another
advantage of being at home is that when I'm not working,
I'm there for them. I don't have to spend time and energy
travelling to and from an office.'

Achieving a balance between work and family is vital for
a working mother, Marie believes. 'If you get the balance
right then you can really enjoy what you're doing. I need to
make sure the children are all all right, to give them time in
the evening, and also to make time for Pat.'

Marie carries the main load of domestic responsibilities,
such as shopping and paying school bills. She switches easily from her businesswoman role to her role as mother. 'I
have no difficulty with that,' she said. 'Well, I've no choice,'
she added, laughing.

'Since I started working, Pat has started appreciating me
more. Up until six years ago, he would have expected his
dinner on the table when he got in. Now, if I'm involved in
a project, he'll help get the dinner ready.

'It's important to maintain your relationship with your
partner,' said Marie. 'I've been fortunate in that I've been
able to grow and develop with Pat and the business. If I had
no involvement in business I would have been left behind in
some respects, especially as the children needed me less.'

IN 1990, Marie and Patrick Cooney appeared on Gay

Byrne's Late Late Show. The high audience figures for the programme assure overnight fame if an interview goes well, which theirs did. Their appearance was the result of Marie's instinct for promoting her product. She would ask RTE to place Tipperary Water strategically on the sets of programmes such as Glenroe, Nighthawks and Fair City – a subliminal and effective form of advertising. 'Whenever you see water in front of the camera, at political conferences and Ard Fheiseanna, for example, you can be sure that somebody has been working behind the scenes to get it there,' she explained.

'I was in RTE one day and was chatting to Gay Byrne's secretary, who found it interesting that I had five children and was also trying to do something for my country. She said she might get in touch some time about going on the show. She phoned that evening to arrange an interview and we were on the show two weeks later. Two million people saw us, and then it went out on Channel 4 in Britain. I was on a high for about three months afterwards. It was incredible publicity. The phone rang nonstop the next day.'

Though never having done a public relations course, Marie has a flair for publicity. She is involved in the sponsorship of the Tipperary hurling team, as well as the race at Drogheda's Bellewstown Races and RTE's Curragh golf day.

After six years in the business she knows the trade inside out. On the export side, she has to handle everything from export documentation to making sure the bottles appear with their correct Greek or Russian labels.

She has recently employed a woman in Cork to help her with the home market. 'I have taken her on to do what I was doing six years ago. She will go to the hotels and restaurants and promote Tipperary Water. We've never done the hotels in Cork before.'

Marie supplies bigger establishments direct. When there are just a few cases involved she gets the customer to order through a wholesaler such as Dublin Foods, with whom she has built up a good relationship. 'Dublin Foods have nicknamed me "Double yellow lines" because I always get them orders where they're likely to get a parking ticket. I helped them build up as I was developing my own business by recommending them to customers, and they in turn have helped me.'

WITH THREE PEOPLE now working exclusively with her, Marie has no intention of ever giving up her central role in the company. 'I would never step out of it. I will carry on indefinitely.'

Marie recently completed a deal with the Jury's hotel group. 'At the moment I'm working on another hotel group. A lot of it is personality. People aren't going to do business with you if you're not nice. The other important thing is to deliver. I have never said I would do something and not done it. I think when a woman is starting she really has to prove herself. She has to deliver. Men can get away with a certain amount. Women can't. We're still at a stage where we have to prove that we can do it. And we can do it, in some instances a lot better than men.'